UML 2.0 in Action

A Project-Based Tutorial

Patrick Grässle
Henriette Baumann
Philippe Baumann

PUBLISHING

BIRMINGHAM - MUMBAI

UML 2.0 in Action
A Project-Based Tutorial

First published: September 2005.

Published by Packt Publishing Ltd.
32 Lincoln Road
Olton
Birmingham, B27 6PA, UK.

ISBN 1-904811-55-8

www.packtpub.com

Cover Design by www.visionwt.com

Authorized translation from the German Edition:

"UML 2.0 projektorientiert"

© 2004 by Galileo Press

GALILEO COMPUTING is an imprint of Galileo Press,

Fort Lee, NJ (USA), Bonn (Germany).

German Edition first published 2004 by Galileo Press.

Credits

Authors

Patrick Grässle

Henriette Baumann

Philippe Baumann

Illustrators

Nilesh Mohite

Dinesh Kandalgaonkar

Cover Designer

Helen Wood

Technical Editor

Chris Smith

Paramita Chakrabarti

Translator

Silvia Saint-Vincent

Proofreader

Chris Smith

Layout

Paramita Chakrabarti

Manjiri Nadkarni

Preface

The advantage of this book lies in its restriction to practical matters. Like many innovative subjects in business computing, the development of technical literature about UML takes place in a highly dynamic manner. The economic interests of producers of relevant tools, of consultants, and of authors are obviously directed towards differentiating every topic and constructing individual opinions. However, this leads to a blurring of the essential advantages—especially with UML. The success of this approach lies in its simplicity, its practicality, and its ability to be integrated. Easily comprehensible and carefully coordinated approaches were developed from real-life problems. These approaches get project parties in different positions, as represented in every project by customer and system-developer, to work together productively on a long-term basis. An excess of methodology is counterproductive because it is only comprehensible to the expert and therefore not widely used.

That is exactly where the authors start. Recognizing the clear advantages of UML, they reduce it to its essential concepts. The authors have the courage to narrow UML appropriately from their own practical experience. The foundation is a pointblank subjective portrayal of their own project experience, which can be confirmed by anyone who has ever attempted professional systems development. Based on this experience, they critically evaluate UML. The result is a handy guide for the use of UML, with countless practice-oriented tips for conquering sub-problems in projects, and checklists to verify goals. The desire is not to present an extensive methodology. On the contrary, the examples are deliberately kept simple, which again helps with the reduction of UML to its essential elements and goals.

Therefore, a project leader who wants to professionally model, coordinate, and control UML projects, won't be able to find solutions for every particular problem in this book. However, it will significantly ease the process of critically evaluating and selecting appropriate literature and tools. For the practice-oriented realist, this book could be the key to solving daily problems.

Prof. Dr. Rainer Thome

Chair of Business Administration and Business Computing,

University of Würzburg.

About the Authors

Patrick Grässle is the co-founder and board member of *KnowGravity Inc.* (www.knowgravity.com) in Zürich, a leading supplier of MDA and Business Rules know-how. Patrick studied Informatics and Economics at the University of Zürich. In 1986, he built his first model of an IT system using structured analysis and did not stop modeling since then. He has applied UML in many projects. He used and consulted structured and object-oriented methods for system specification. In the nineties, he helped develop the first localized UML trainings in Switzerland.

The UML-based 'Model Driven Architecture' and the 'Business Rules Approach' absorb his main interest nowadays, but he is still doing UML training and consulting. Patrick can be reached at patrick.graessle@knowgravity.com.

Henriette Baumann is the co-founder and board member of *integratio GmbH* (www.integratio.com), based in Zurich. Henriette studied Informatics and Economics and was involved in software development and engineering since the mid-eighties, particularly with the transformation of business requirements in software systems. In 1998, she started with UML business modeling and has used UML in several projects. Today her main focus is on project management and consulting for business analysis, business requirements engineering, and business specifications based on UML, especially for financial service companies.

Henriette can be reached at henriette.baumann@integratio.com.

Philippe Baumann is co-founder and member of the board of *integratio GmbH* (www.integratio.com), based in Zurich.

Philippe studied Informatics at the University of Hagen (D) and was involved in software development and application integration since the mid-eighties. In 1998, he started with UML, and its usage in system integration and electronic data interchange between companies.

Today he is the project manager and consultant for technical aspects and implementation of software integration using UML. He is also active in the field of implementation and integration of Open Source business software such as ERP and CRM.

Philippe can be reached at philippe.baumann@integratio.com.

Table of Contents

About This Book

The *OMG Specification* states:

> "The Unified Modeling Language (UML) is a graphical language for visualizing, specifying, constructing, and documenting the artifacts of a software-intensive system."

Modeling is an essential part of large software projects, which also helps in the development of medium and small projects. UML can be used to model a variety of systems: software systems, business systems, or any other system. With its changes and extensions, UML 2.0 now supports the modeling of business processes much better.

What This Book Covers

This book shows how, with UML, simple models of business processes and specification models can be created and read with little effort. Most books deal with UML almost in its entirety. However, often lack of time, previous knowledge, or motivation to deal with the topic with the necessary intensity prevents us from understanding the material completely and putting it into action. This book is meant for exactly these cases. It presents UML only partially and in a simplified manner. We put together those parts of UML whose application has proven to be practical.

Chapter 1 introduces us to UML and lists the advantages of using UML as a Modeling Language. *Chapter 2* introduces us to the case study. The purpose of choosing a case study is to provide a coherent example through the chapters of this book. The chapter also explains several basic terms and concepts like models, views, diagrams, information systems, methods, and notations. The models and views provided by this book help choose the most suitable model for a requirement specification.

Chapter 3 discusses the construction of business system models. It explains the benefits of the different views in a business system and discusses the elements of each view. It also provides instructions about how to construct use case diagrams.

Chapter 4 illustrates how a conceptual model of an IT system can be developed with the help of UML. *Chapter 5* describes the integration of the IT system into its environment. It discusses how to model the messages that are exchanged between the various IT systems, and the processes that are necessary to exchange these messages.

Conventions

In this book, you will find a number of styles of text that distinguish between different kinds of information. Here are some examples of these styles, and an explanation of their meaning.

New terms and **important words** are introduced in a bold-type font. Words that you see on the screen, in menus or dialog boxes for example, appear in our text like this: "clicking the Next button moves you to the next screen".

Tips, suggestions, or important notes appear in a box like this.

Reader Feedback

Feedback from our readers is always welcome. Let us know what you think about this book, what you liked or may have disliked. Reader feedback is important for us to develop titles that you really get the most out of.

To send us general feedback, simply drop an e-mail to feedback@packtpub.com, making sure to mention the book title in the subject of your message.

If there is a book that you need and would like to see us publish, please send us a note in the SUGGEST A TITLE form on www.packtpub.com or e-mail title@packtpub.com.

If there is a topic that you have expertise in and you are interested in either writing or contributing to a book, see our author guide on www.packtpub.com/authors.

Customer Support

Now that you are the proud owner of a Packt book, we have a number of things to help you to get the most from your purchase.

Errata

Although we have taken every care to ensure the accuracy of our contents, mistakes do happen. If you find a mistake in one of our books—maybe a mistake in text or code—we would be grateful if you would report this to us. By doing this you can save other readers from frustration, and help to improve subsequent versions of this book.

If you find any errata, report them by visiting http://www.packtpub.com/support, selecting your book, clicking on the Submit Errata link, and entering the details of your errata. Once your errata have been verified, your submission will be accepted and the errata added to the list of existing errata. The existing errata can be viewed by selecting your title from http://www.packtpub.com/support.

Questions

You can contact us at questions@packtpub.com if you are having a problem with some aspect of the book, and we will do our best to address it.

1

Introduction

I'm still confused, but on a much higher level.

Unified Modeling Language (UML) makes it possible to describe systems with words and pictures. It can be used to model a variety of systems: software systems, business systems, or any other system. Especially notable are the various graphical charts—use case diagrams with their stick figures or the widely used class diagrams. While these diagrams aren't fundamentally new, the worldwide unification of modeling languages is new with UML, which was standardized by the **Object Management Group (OMG)**, an international association that promotes open standards for object-oriented applications (http://www.omg.org).

Most books about UML describe it almost in its entirety. However, our experience has shown that in reality there is often a lack of time, previous knowledge, or motivation to deal with the topic with the necessary intensity. In these cases, the material can't be completely understood and put into action. This book is meant for exactly these cases. We put together those parts of UML whose application has proven to be practical. With a little effort, anybody should be able to make use of UML.

There are several reasons to use UML as a modeling language:

- The unification of terminology and the standardization of notation lead to a significant easing of communication for all parties involved. It facilitates the exchange of models between different departments or companies. Moreover, it eases the transfer of projects between project teams or project team members.

- UML grows as the requirements for modeling grow. Because UML is a powerful modeling language, you can start with the development of simple models or model complex systems in great detail. If the basic functionality of UML is not sufficient, you can extend it through the use of stereotypes.

- UML builds upon widely used and proven approaches. UML was not devised in an ivory tower but was developed mainly from real-world problems and existing modeling languages. This guarantees usability and real-life functionality.
- UML is widely supported.
- UML-based bids for software systems can be compared much more easily.

This book is based on UML version 2.0, as adopted by the Object Management Group "(*OMG Unified Modeling Language*: *Superstructure, Version 2.0, Revised Final Adopted Specification, October 2004*", from `http://www.omg.org`).

At the time this book was printed, standardization of UML was not fully completed. However, subsequent changes to UML 2.0 will not affect the simplified approach that our book presents.

Our book was written for computer scientists and for people involved in the development process of IT systems, such as analysts, decision makers, users, and experts. It shows how, with UML, simple models of business processes and specification models can be created and read with little effort. Our experience with projects showed that:

- Often only components of a model are created.
- Most of the time the entire system is *not* modeled.
- Very little time is spent on training in modeling language and methodology.
- In short: modeling is not given much priority.

Certainly a few projects use the complete UML model appropriately. However, the bulk of all projects use UML or other modeling languages, modeling tools, and modeling methods to only a small degree, if at all. While enthusiasm and motivation are strong at the beginning of the project, modeling and documentation of the modeling results are often the first to fall victim to the increasing time pressure as the deadline approaches.

Unfortunately, we cannot change that. Considering these circumstances, we have tried to portray a much-simplified picture of UML, in order to make it possible to use UML more efficiently and appropriately with only a small investment of time.

Experience shows that mastering only a few elements of UML leads to better results than the superficial knowledge of many UML elements. So we have selected some of these elements for you—subjectively, of course. We have not even mentioned many elements of UML, and explain others in a very simplified manner. Even though that is not always how it was originally intended, it does reflect our practical experience.

With its changes and extensions, UML 2.0 supports the modeling of business processes much better. The increased size of UML 2.0's vocabulary shows that it's no longer sufficient to define only certain elements of the language, but also necessary to define the use of UML in specialized fields, such as, system integration or data warehousing.

In this book we have emphasized these aspects through the use of profiles, while defining the language elements (vocabulary/terminology) of UML 2.0. We will refer to these profiles at the appropriate places throughout this book.

We have structured this book so that it can be read while working on a project. We begin with the modeling of a business system and its business processes in Chapter 3, *Modeling Business Systems*. Then we go on to specify an IT system that is to be embedded into the business system (Chapter 4, *Modeling IT Systems*) and lastly describe the integration of the IT system into its environment (Chapter 5, *Modeling for System Integration*). These three chapters are independent entities. You can read only those chapters that you require for your project. But in any case, you should first read Chapter 2, *Basic Principles and Background*, where we introduce the case study. This chapter also explains several basic terms and concepts that the following chapters build on.

We use a case study throughout this book to convey the theoretical knowledge about UML. This case study serves the sole purpose of illustrating UML, since much can be explained and understood through the use of examples rather than abstract definitions. The reader is supposed to get a 'feel' for UML. Of course it is not possible to use every diagram and every piece of documentation of the entire case study: that would have been well beyond the scope of this book and is not necessary for the comprehension of UML. The case study—passenger services at the fictional UML Airport—does not always accurately represent real passenger services: we have simplified it in parts. However, this does not have a negative effect on understanding UML.

This book does not assume any prior knowledge of UML or object-oriented programming. However, a basic understanding of the development of IT systems is expected.

At this point, we especially want to thank the friendly employees of Unique Zurich Airport, who helped us with patience and competence to understand the technical details of our case study. We thank everyone who helped with the creation and revision of this book. In particular, we want to thank the editor of our German edition, Judith Stevens-Lemoine, and her team at Galileo for their competent and friendly attention. We also found helpful the critical comments and suggestions from our readers, and our colleagues at Integratio and KnowGravity. Last, but not least, we want to thank everyone who bought a copy of the first two German editions of *UML 2.0 in Action: A Project-Based Tutorial*. Thanks to you, this revised version was made possible.

Henriette and Philippe Baumann and Patrick Grässle.

2

Basic Principles and Background

Much of what will be explained in the next few chapters is based on a few fundamental concepts. These have been summarized in this chapter.

2.1 Introduction to the Case Study

For our case study we have chosen an airport—the UML Airport. Anyone who has ever been on a flight will have no problems understanding our example.

We will restrict our example to those areas of the airport that passengers are in contact with during departure, meaning we will take a closer look at **passenger check-in** and **boarding**. Figure 2.1 illustrates how passenger services can be distinguished from other areas of the airport. It shows the various stages that passengers go through until they are seated in the airplane, buckled up, and the plane is ready to take off. Not all stages passengers go through are related to passenger services. The stages that belong to passenger services are framed and printed in italic font.

A sequence of steps like this is called a **scenario**. However, the depicted scenario is only one of many possible scenarios. The following exceptions are possible for passenger check-in and boarding:

- The passenger only has carry-on luggage.
- The passenger doesn't buy anything at the newsstand.
- The passenger is running late and now has to check in as quickly as possible.
- The passenger loses his or her boarding pass.
- The passenger arrived by plane and merely has to change planes, meaning that he or she doesn't leave the transit area.

- The passenger checks in, but falls asleep on an uncomfortable chair in the waiting area, and misses the departure of his or her flight, despite being called repeatedly.
- The passenger doesn't get through passport inspection because his or her passport has expired.

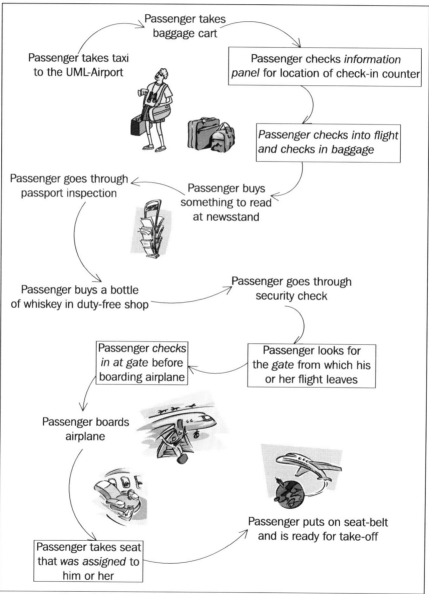

Figure 2.1 Case Study: "Passenger takes plane to go on vacation"

Think about which of the above-mentioned scenarios are relevant for passenger departure and whether there are more relevant scenarios than those mentioned.

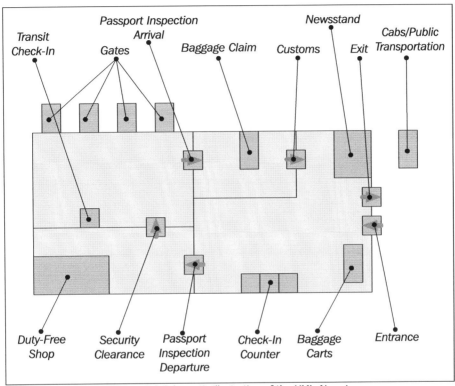

Figure 2.2 Schematic illustration of the UML Airport

The schematic illustration of the UML Airport in Figure 2.2 should help you to understand the events of the case study better. Many areas around the main passenger services are related in one or more ways to passenger services. Some examples are:

- Ticket sales
- Newsstand
- Duty-free shop
- Passport inspection/immigration
- Flight control
- Information desk
- Baggage check-in and transportation

Passenger services have to exchange data with some of these areas. They also have to communicate with other areas of the airport. We will introduce those areas when we discuss business models and models of system integration. Therefore, the case study will be expanded further in the following chapters.

UML Airport is a small airport and the case study has been purposely kept simple. Anyone who has ever been on a flight should be able to understand the examples.

The purpose of the case study is to provide a coherent example throughout the chapters of this book. A few details of the case study require further explanation:

- The plane ticket consists of the actual ticket and up to four additional sections. The **ticket** is the little booklet that has a separate coupon for every part of the trip. For example, a ticket could contain a coupon for the flight from Zurich to Frankfurt, one for the flight from Frankfurt to London, and one for the return flight from London to Zurich. Each time at check-in the appropriate coupon will be exchanged for a boarding pass. The ticket always stays with the passenger.

- We distinguish between a flight and a flight number. For instance, a **flight number** could be LH435 or LX016. It stands for a regular flight that occurs at a certain time from the departure airport to the destination airport. A **flight**, on the other hand, would be, for example, LH435 on 26th August, 2000. It is, so to speak, an execution of a flight number. A flight could be canceled due to bad weather. A flight number is used as long as the airline offers a certain flight regularly.

- We differentiate between three options for check-in:
  - **Normal check-in** with luggage at a normal check-in counter
  - **Express check-in** without luggage at a special check-in counter
  - **Automated check-in** without luggage at a machine

2.2 Models, Views, and Diagrams

2.2.1 What is a Model?

Models are often built in the context of business and IT systems in order to better understand existing or future systems. However, a model never fully corresponds to reality. Modeling always means **emphasizing** and **omitting**: emphasizing essential details and omitting irrelevant ones. But what is essential and what is irrelevant? There is no universal answer to this question. Rather, the answer depends on **what** the goals of the model are and **who** is viewing or reading it.

Think about what is emphasized or omitted in the following models:

- A wind tunnel model of a car

- A model of a building scaled at 1:50

- A route plan of the subway

- A map

- An organization chart

The more information a model is supposed to give, the more complex and difficult it becomes. A map of Europe, for example, that simultaneously contains political, geological, demographic, and transportation-related information is hardly legible. The solution to this problem is to convey the different types of information on individual maps. **Different views** are formed of the objects under consideration. These views are interconnected in many ways. Generally, if one view is changed, all other views have to be adjusted as well. If, for instance, in the Netherlands new land is reclaimed from the North Sea, all views—meaning all maps—have to be updated.

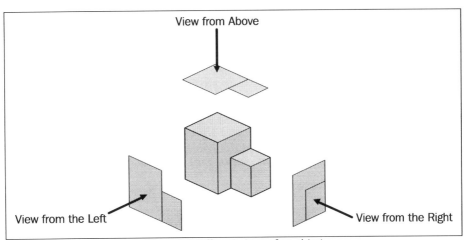

Figure 2.3 Different views of an object

The same is true for the model of a building. If a new wing is added to an existing building various views are affected, including the floor plan, the different exterior views, and the 3D-model made from wood. Figure 2.3 illustrates this in a schematic manner. In Section 2.4, *The Models of our Case Study*, we specifically address the relationships between the models we use in this book. The different views within each model are described in more detail in Chapter 3, *Modeling Business Systems*; Chapter 4, *Modeling IT Systems*; and Chapter 5, *Modeling for System Integration*.

2.2.2 Why do we Need Models?

As a general rule, a model of a system has to perform the following tasks:

- **Communication** between all involved parties: In order to build the right system, it is essential that all involved parties think along the same lines. It is particularly important that everyone understands the terminology used, that customers agree upon the same requirements, that developers understand these requirements, and that the decisions made can still be understood months later.

- **Visualization** of all facts for customers, experts, and users: All accumulated facts relevant to the system need to be presented in such a way that everyone concerned can understand them. However, according to our real-life experience, we often hit a wall of resistance when we want to communicate with diagrams instead of text. It is necessary to overcome this resistance. Behind it is often a fear of the unknown; and the diagrams might look a bit complicated at first. Therefore, this book contains directions on how to read each diagram.

- **Verification** of facts in terms of completeness, consistency, and correctness: A (more or less) formal model makes it possible to verify the facts obtained for completeness, consistency, and correctness. In particular, the clear depiction of interrelationships makes it possible to ask specific questions, and to answer them. We will list these questions with each diagram.

Answer the following questions for yourself:

- When was the last time you felt that you were at cross-purposes when you discussed a system?

- When was the last time you felt that you were discussing the same issue over and over again?

- When was the last time you wished that the consensus you reached during a discussion had been recorded?

2.2.3 Purpose and Target Group of a Model

In real life we often observe that the results of cumbersome, tedious, and expensive modeling simply disappear in a stack of paper on someone's desk. We might ask why this is so. Two factors greatly influence the result of modeling: **for whom** do we create the model and for **what purpose** is it supposed to be used. If we don't discuss and define these aspects sufficiently, we run the risk of creating models that don't contain what is important to the user. In other words, if details are not emphasized and omitted appropriately, the model is rendered worthless.

To define the purpose and target group the following questions should be answered:

- How much **business expertise** can we expect? Can we assume basic knowledge of the subject, or do we have to explain the fundamentals of the model's events and processes?

- What amount of **detail** does the target group need? What level of complexity does the model permit? If processes and systems are subject to constant changes, a highly detailed model might be unrealistic. This is because, most of the time, it is not possible to maintain those models in a satisfactory manner. A less detailed model requires less effort to develop and update, but it is also less precise.

- How much **time** does the target group have to read and interpret the model? Prevent your model from disappearing in a stack of paper on someone's desk by choosing the appropriate level of detail and complexity; otherwise, nobody might have enough time to read it.

- What **language** can be used in the model? Does the target group understand technical business terms? Do they understand IT terminology?
  Let's clarify with an easy example: If a bottle filled with water is labeled 'water', virtually anyone who can read will understand the bottle's content. However, if the bottle is labeled 'H_2O'—even though this is correct—we reach a much smaller group of people, for example, the workers of a chemistry lab. Yet, the additional benefit is that it shows the composition of the content: hydrogen and oxygen. In either case, you will have to decide what 'label' is most appropriate for your target group.

- What level of **abstraction** should you choose? The less abstract a model, the more comprehensible, and clear it is for the user. This is because a less abstract model is closer to the user's actual use and language. On the other hand, models with a high level of abstraction are more reusable and they are more easily converted into IT systems. We can also prove more accurately that they are correct. IT specialists probably manage highly abstract models best. Users, on the other hand, might pull their hair out if asked to deal with a model like that.

Practical Tips

Compromises have to be made between the level of abstraction, clarity, and the amount of detail used for a model. It is possible to develop several model components, differing in degree of formality and detail, in order to satisfy different target groups. In this way communication between model builders, customers, users, and developers can be facilitated much more easily. It is important not to 'overdo' it, but to adjust the model to its target groups and their uses.

Analysis or design **patterns** are example models that describe common design and modeling methods. You should, whenever possible, look for these example models: on the Internet, in books (for example, Martin Fowler: *Analysis Patterns: Reusable Object Models*, Addison-Wesley, 1999), in magazines, or ask your coworkers.

2.2.4 Process of Analysis

Figure 2.4 shows the process of analysis, which consists of **obtaining**, **representing**, and **verifying facts**:

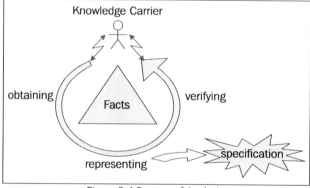

Figure 2.4 Process of Analysis

This is the job of the analyst. The process of analysis produces a specification that comes from the model and other representations. The analyst works with knowledge carriers, such as customers, users, and domain experts:

- Facts are **obtained** by collaboration between analysts and domain experts in which knowledge carriers contribute domain knowledge and analysts contribute methodological knowledge.

- Facts are **represented** in diagrams and documents, which are usually prepared by the analyst.

- Facts are **verified** only by knowledge carriers, since they alone can decide if the presented facts are correct. Verification is absolutely essential. Without it we might have pretty diagrams, but the probability is high that the facts represented are faulty. In simple terms: development of a model without verification is absolutely worthless!

Practical Tips

It is impossible to develop and verify a usable model without mastering the technical foundations of a topic. Where do we find these **knowledge carriers** who know something about the systems that we want to model? We have had good experiences with the following groups of people:

- People who are involved in performing, operating, and controlling business processes
- Users of similar or related IT systems
- Customers, who are often critical and creative knowledge carriers
- Business Partners
- Domain Experts
- Management
- External Observers

Several helpful techniques have proven to be useful for the analysis and understanding of business processes:

- Observing employees at work
- Participating in the investigated business processes
- Taking the role of an outsider (e.g. of a customer)
- Carrying out surveys
- Conducting interviews
- Brainstorming with everyone involved
- Discussing with domain experts
- Reviewing existing forms, documentation, specifications, handbooks, and work tools
- Describing the organizational structure and workflow management (organization charts, etc.)

2.2.5 Diagrams as Views

Each particular UML diagram corresponds to one **view** of a model of a system. Depending on the type of diagram used, different aspects are either emphasized or omitted. All the different views combined result in a good model of a system. Most of the UML diagrams are **graphs** (as shown in Figure 2.5), implying that they consist of elements that are connected through lines:

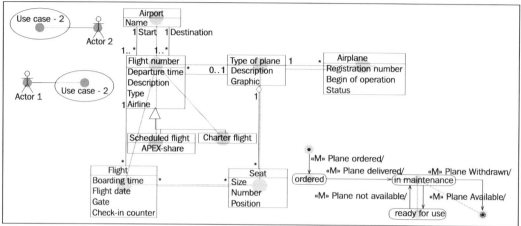

Figure 2.5 Diagram as graphs

To read diagrams, you have to know what types of elements and lines are allowed and what they mean. We'll explain this for the diagrams we use in the following chapters.

Even **computer-aided software engineering (CASE)** tools treat UML diagrams as views. They use a **database** in which the information about the model is stored. Each diagram shows—as a view—a part of that information. In this way, the CASE tool helps to preserve the consistency of each view. If, for example, the name of a class is changed in a class diagram, the statechart diagram of that class is automatically updated:

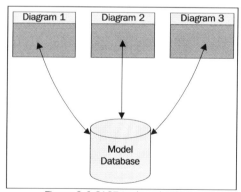

Figure 2.6 CASE tool as database

The model database is what fundamentally differentiates a CASE tool from a graphical program (Figure 2.6). Any UML diagram can be generated easily with paper and pencil or a graphical program. In this case, however, the various diagrams are nothing more than drawings. Only the use of a CASE tool with a database, according to UML specifications, permits consistent collection, management, and modification of model information. UML provides its own database model: the UML meta-model, a component of the UML specifications ("*OMG: Unified Modeling Language: Infrastructure, Version 2.0, Final Adopted Specification*, September 2003, and *OMG: Unified Modeling Language: Superstructure, Version 2.0, Revised Final Adopted Specification*, October 2004": http://www.omg.org). All elements found in UML diagrams, as well as the descriptions of these elements, are contained in the UML meta-model. It states, for example, that a class can have attributes and methods. This "data model" of UML as a language, is the foundation of the model databases of all UML CASE tools. Unfortunately, many CASE tools are hungry for resources, expensive, poorly developed, cumbersome, and require extensive training. Despite this, except for very small projects, their use is worthwhile.

2.3 Information Systems and IT Systems

In almost all occupations, part of the job is dealing with information. It has been this way for thousands of years and is one of the reasons behind the development of writing. Some of the oldest texts found in Europe include, for instance, stock lists from the palace of Knossos in Crete. If we were able to watch the stock managers work as they did 3,500 years ago, we could probably map the business processes that people followed back then. We could see that these people were dealing with suppliers and buyers, that they were exchanging goods, and that they kept written records of their business activities. The same was true for a Roman olive merchant 1,500 years later, for a Hanseatic merchant's trading office in fifteenth century Northern Germany, or at Lloyd's of London at the beginning of the last century.

In the above examples, more or less complex information systems were used to handle daily tasks. The purpose of these information systems was, and is, to manage the information needed to operate a business. Of course, all of this took place without computers. Information systems were supported by other techniques such as chalkboards, large filing systems, and index cards. Today, computers allow us to implement information systems as IT systems. This creates new possibilities that would probably be unthinkable for the Roman olive merchant. But basically, the point is still to provide and to process data that is needed for dealing with everyday business processes. We will generally be talking about IT systems in this book, since we assume that information systems modeled with UML are implemented by IT technology.

In our case study—**passenger services** at UML Airport—employees at the check-in deal with passengers, plane tickets, and flights that are real. On the other hand, there is a representation or **image** of these passengers, plane tickets, and flights in the information system. These images consist of **information** about the passengers, tickets, and flights stored in the information system, needed for operating processes, as shown in Figure 2.7:

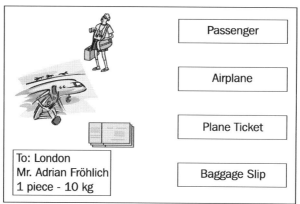

Figure 2.7 Objects from the real world and their images

An **IT system** is a computer-based system—a system that provides information needed for the execution of certain business processes, generally in response to a query by a user. Of course the IT system has to be 'fed' with information, so that it can answer queries.

Figure 2.8 shows the cooperation between business systems and IT systems schematically. Within the framework of the business processes of a business system, information is retrieved from and stored in IT systems:

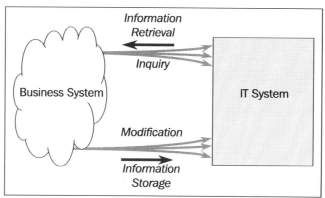

Figure 2.8 IT System

The modeling techniques introduced in this book not only hold true for the development of IT systems, but they can also be used whenever an information system needs to be analyzed. To illustrate this, we invented a second example—in addition to our case study on passenger services at UML Airport—which we will come back to in different places of this book.

The second example is a medieval Hanseatic merchant's trading office owned by a Mr. Hafenstein. (The Hanseatic League was a powerful alliance of merchant guilds in cities of Northern Germany and the Baltic that controlled trade in this region during the middle ages.) The supervisor of the office is the faithful and diligent secretary Hildebrandt. The office keeps several books, namely a daybook, a sales ledger, and a customer index. Each book is the responsibility of a different clerk. Nobody besides the clerk responsible is allowed to make any changes in a book, and only he knows exactly where in the book a particular piece of information is recorded.

In our terminology, the office, including Hildebrandt, the clerks, and the books, make up the information system. With the help of this example we want to show in different places in this book that, even though an information system *can* be implemented as an IT system with the help of computer technology, conceptually it has nothing to do with computers. Instead, it can be realized in many ways.

2.4 The Models of our Case Study

In our case study we construct three models of different systems:

1. The model of the business system describes passenger services, meaning the business surroundings of the IT system. It deals with business processes, passengers, business partners, employees, etc. We discuss this model in Chapter 3, *Modeling Business Systems*.

2. The model of the IT system explains the IT system that was built for passenger services. The model of the passenger service business system serves as the foundation for the model of the IT system. We discuss this model in Chapter 4, *Modeling IT Systems*.

3. The model of system integration describes integration into the environment, especially gateways to the outside world. Here also, the model of the passenger service business system serves as the foundation. This model is discussed in Chapter 5, *Modeling for System Integration*:

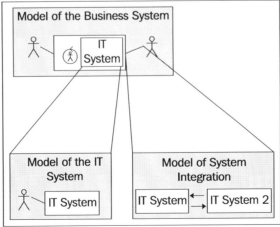

Figure 2.9 Models of the case study

All three models are needed to build and integrate IT systems; the model of the IT system alone is insufficient. This is true not only for our case study, but also for all other cases.

You can see in Figure 2.9 that the model of the business system provides the foundation for all other models. In this way, it constitutes the basis to work from for everyone involved in the project. Because of this, it is of great advantage to use a **unified modeling language**, which can be understood by people from the different departments as well as from information technology. This enables a smooth exchange of models between the various areas. It also significantly eases verification of the models. We are convinced that UML functions as a link that has the ability to close the existing gap between the technical requirements and the actual performance characteristics of IT systems.

2.5 History of UML: Methods and Notations

In its short history, information technology has already produced a plethora of **methods and notations**. We have methods and notations for design, structure, processing, and storage of information. We also have methods for the planning, modeling, implementation, assembly, testing, documentation, adjustment, etc. of systems. Some of the concepts used are relatively fundamental, and because of that, they can also be found beyond the field of information technology. One example of that is inheritance, which is present in nature, but is also a cornerstone of object-oriented programming.

Until about the 1970s, software developers viewed the development of software as an artistic venture. But because systems became more and more complex, software development and maintenance could no longer be conquered with this creative-individual approach. Eventually, this approach led to the **software crisis**.

This crisis leads to the **engineering approach** (software engineering) and structured programming. Methods were developed for the structuring of systems and for the processes of design, development, and maintenance. Process-oriented approaches, for example the **Hierarchy Input Processing Output (HIPO)** method, emphasized the functionality of systems. With this method the total system is divided into smaller components through functional decomposition.

Figure 2.10 gives a visual overview (hierarchical diagram) of the sub-functions in the invoice example. An input-process-output schema describes every functional element.

At the same time, data-structure oriented approaches were developed, such as the Jackson method, in which the program structure is derived from the graphical display of data structures.

Figure 2.11 shows, in the left-hand column, the structure of an inventory data set. The right-hand column shows the program structure that was derived from the data structure:

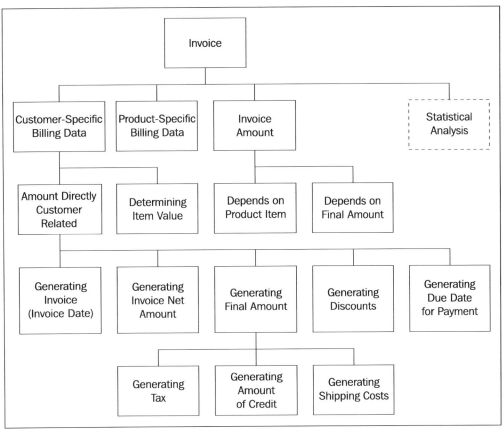

Figure 2.10 HIPO diagram

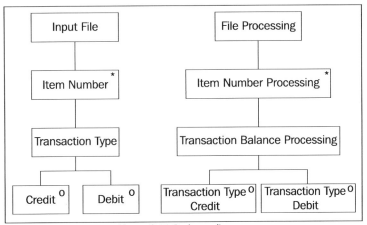

Figure 2.11 Jackson diagram

In all these methods and notations, we split the system into two portions—a data section and a procedure section. This is clearly recognizable in older programming languages such as COBOL. Data flow-charts, structure charts, HIPO diagrams, and Jackson diagrams are used to illustrate the range of functions. Naturally, these early methods emphasized the development of new systems.

In the 1980s, classical structural analysis was developed further. Developers generated entity relationship diagrams for data modeling and Petri nets for process modeling.

As systems became more complex, no longer could every system be designed "from scratch". Properties, such as maintainability and re-usability, became more and more important. Object-oriented programming languages were developed, and with them, the first object-oriented modeling languages emerged in the 1970s and 1980s. In the 1990s, the first publications on object-oriented analysis and object-oriented design became available to the public. In the mid-1990s, already more than 50 object-oriented methods existed, as well as just as many design formats. A **unified** modeling language seemed indispensable.

At the beginning of the 1990s, the object-oriented methods of Grady Booch and James Rumbaugh were widely used. In October 1994, the Rational Software Corporation (part of IBM since February 2003) began the creation of a unified modeling language. First, they agreed upon a standardization of notation (language), since this seemed less elaborate than the standardization of methods. In doing so, they integrated the **Booch Method** of Grady Booch, the **Object Modeling Technique (OMT)** by James Rumbaugh, and **Object-Oriented Software Engineering (OOSE)**, by Ivar Jacobsen, with elements of other methods and published this new notation under the name **UML**, version 0.9. The goal was not to formulate a completely new notation, but to adapt, to expand, and to simplify the existing and accepted types of diagrams of several object-oriented methods, such as class diagrams, Jacobson's Use Case Diagrams, or Harel's Statechart Diagrams. The means of representation that were used in structured methods were applied to UML. Thus, UML's activity diagrams are, for example, influenced by the make-up of data flow charts and Petri nets.

What is outstanding and new in UML is not its content, but its standardization to a single unified language with formally defined meaning.

Well-known companies, such as IBM, Oracle, Microsoft, Digital, Hewlett-Packard, and Unisys were included in the further development of UML. In 1997, UML version 1.1 was submitted to and approved by the OMG. UML version 1.2, with editorial adaptations, was released in 1998, followed by version 1.3 a year later, and UML 1.5 in March, 2003. Developers had already been working on version 2.0 of UML since the year 2000, and it was approved as a Final Adopted Specification by OMG in June, 2003. When this book went to print in June, 2005 the final stage of adoption by OMG as an **Available Specification** was not yet completed.

2.6 Requirement Specification

Models of the system to be developed make up an integral part of every requirement specification. This book provides a substantiated basis for the development of these models. Unfortunately, there is no universal recipe for the specification of requirements. Rather, the choice and level of detail of models depend on various factors. Our experience shows that the following three points are most important:

- Who is specifying?
- For whom is it being specified?
- What is being specified?

2.6.1 Guidance for Decision Making

The models and views that are provided by this book are basically the building blocks from which you can choose the required models for a requirement specification. The following table will support you in making the proper choice of models and views:

Model (What)	View	Originator (Who)	Target Audience (for Whom)	Purpose (for What)
Business System	External View	User Agent	User Agent	Business Documentation
			IT Agent	Basis for IT System Specification
	Internal View	User Agent	User Agent	Business Documentation, Description of Procedures
			IT Agent	Basis for IT System Specification
IT System	External View	User Agent	IT Agent User Agent	Requirements of an IT System
	Structural View	IT Agent	IT Agent	IT System Specification
	Performance View	User Agent IT Agent	IT Agent	IT System Specification
	Interaction View	User Agent IT Agent	IT Agent	IT System Specification

Model (What)	View	Originator (Who)	Target Audience (for Whom)	Purpose (for What)
System Integration	Process View	User Agent	IT Agent	IT System Integration Specification
	Static View	IT Agent	IT Agent	IT System Integration Specification

2.6.2 Verification

All the views introduced in this book describe a model that documents the requirements from the viewpoint of the user. This means that all utilized models and views:

- Can only be created in cooperation with user agents
- Can only be verified by user agents with respect to correctness of content

Even though we develop the model of the IT system for the target audience, the IT agents, we cannot do so without user agents, who have to provide the requirements and verify the model. They represent the user's point of view and are knowledge carriers of the user domain.

Since various groups are involved in the development and verification of requirement specifications, it is especially important to use a unified modeling language, in order to prevent misunderstanding though misinterpretation.

2.7 UML 2.0

2.7.1 Overview of UML 2.0

UML 2.0 in Action: *A Project-Based Tutorial* is based on the new version of UML—UML 2.0. In this version, the structure and documentation of UML was completely revised. There are now two documents available that describe UML:

- *UML 2.0 Infrastructure* defines the basic constructs of the language on which UML is based. This section is not directly relevant to the users of UML (our readers), but is directed more towards the developers of modeling tools.
- *UML 2.0 Superstructure* defines the user constructs of UML 2.0, meaning those elements of UML that users work with at the immediate level.

Among other things, this revision of UML was created to pursue the following goals:

- To restructure and refine UML so that usability, implementation, and adaptation are simplified.
- The UML infrastructure is supposed to:
  - Provide a reusable meta-language core, with which UML can define itself
  - Provide mechanisms for the adjustment of language
- The UML superstructure is supposed to:
  - Feature better support for component-based development
  - Improve constructs for the specification of architecture
  - Provide better options for the modeling of behavior

In addition to the proposal of UML Infrastructure and UML Superstructure specifications, separate proposals were published for a new **Object Constraint Language (OCL)** as well as for Diagram Interchange. Together, they make up the complete UML 2.0 package, as shown in Figure 2.12:

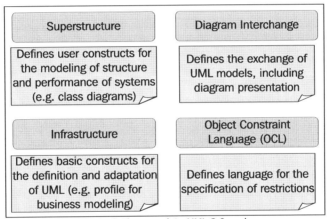

Figure 2.12 The complete UML 2.0 package

UML 2.0, as a whole, is more extensive and more complex than earlier versions. The extent of UML documentation has also further increased. While the documentation of UML 1.5, including OCL, comprised about 730 pages, the documentation of UML 2.0, also including OCL, contains approximately 1050 pages.

Even though part of the documentation doesn't concern the 'normal' UML user, for a member of a software development project, reading the complete work is unrealistic. This is not only due to the number of pages, but also because of the number and complexity of UML constructs. Because of this, reduction to the UML constructs necessary for everyday project work is even more necessary than with earlier versions.

From this follow two conclusions for our book *UML 2.0 in Action*: *A Project-Based Tutorial*.

The concept of this book is to show a very simplified picture of UML. This is becoming even more important with the increasing scope of UML, since the accessibility of UML did not become any greater with version 2.0.

Fortunately, many of the new features of UML 2.0 have little or no influence at the level of detail used in this book. Consequently, there are only a few changes compared to the earlier German editions of *UML 2.0 in Action*: *A Project-Based Tutorial*. The restricted scope of our book ensures stability towards the changes in new UML versions.

We consciously only show the tip of the iceberg, while the part hidden under water becomes bigger and bigger. More than ever, we are of the opinion that the tip of the iceberg (as shown in Figure 2.13) is sufficient for our target audience—members of IT project teams—to understand UML enough to use it meaningfully in projects:

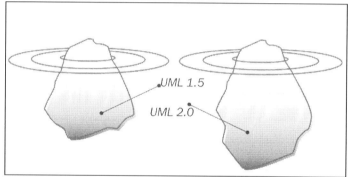

Figure 2.13 The UML iceberg

We would also like to point out a new possibility that UML 2.0 opens up. One of the goals of UML 2.0 was the definition of formal and completely defined semantics. If this new possibility is utilized for the development of models, corresponding systems can be generated from these models. This yields the following advantages:

- A model that was described with UML reflects the real system.
- It is possible to correct mistakes in the model early and continuously.
- Intermediate steps such as amending code outside of the model design are omitted.
- It is possible to make the same model executable on different platforms (hardware as well as software).

However, a price has to be paid for these advantages. It becomes necessary to acquire a deep and accurate understanding of UML and considerable effort has to be invested in the development of the models.

2.7.2 Effects on the Business System Model

Some changes made in performance modeling enhanced the possibilities for modeling business systems. First, we'll give examples of several of the changes and improvements.

Activity diagrams are no longer special cases of the statechart diagram. Initially, this fact was not relevant for the normal UML user. However, in addition to the new autonomy in the meta-model, several other changes and improvements were made:

Until now, the separate steps in the activity diagram were referred to as activities. Now the entire diagram is called an **activity**, whereas the steps previously called activities are now referred to as **actions**. An action can call a primary operation as well as another activity. This enables flexible modulation in the top-down view of models.

A division does not necessarily have to be re-synchronized.

An activity can have more than one initial state. With this, several events can be started at the same time.

Input and output parameters can be added to an activity.

One of the improvements made in the sequence diagram is the addition of so-called **operators**. These operators make it possible to package several actions/activities within a sequence diagram. For instance, operators can be used to refer to other sequence diagrams or individual sequences. Appropriate operators can also represent iterations. With the newly introduced operators, sequence diagrams now support a top-down view.

OCL is now an inherent part of UML. It can be used to describe agreements, invariants, preconditions, and post conditions within UML models, which enables more precise modeling of business systems and business processes.

2.7.3 Effects on the IT System Model

The diagrams that we have used in this book in the different views of the IT system did not undergo any significant changes.

The biggest change occurred in the notation of the sequence diagram. Here, among other things, the interaction reference is available as a construct for modularization. However, nothing changed concerning the meaning and functionality of sequence diagrams at the level of detail used in this book. The same holds true for the class diagram and the case diagram.

Statechart diagrams underwent the most interesting changes for the modeling of IT systems: connection points allow, for example, better modulation of statechart diagrams. However, we decided not to use this language element in our simplified approach to UML.

2.7.4 Effects on the Systems Integration Model

Of course, the improvements in behavioral modeling also had an effect on the process view in the systems integration model. A significant improvement is the ability to add input and output parameters to activities (see Section 2.7.2, *Effects on the Business System Model*).

Hardly any changes were made in the area of static views, meaning the design of business objects with class diagrams.

In addition to the changes that were made within the framework of UML 2.0, the UML profile for **Enterprise Application Integration (EAI)** is of increasing importance in the field of system integration. Besides the basic operations needed in the field of system integration, it shows the data meta-models of various programming languages that are not object-oriented. However, this occurs at a more detailed level, which has no influence upon this text.

2.7.5 Conclusion

For the normal user, UML 2.0 does not turn the previous versions of UML upside down, but represents an improvement on existing concepts. It is probably wise to use UML 2.0 for future models. On the other hand, it should be possible to continue using existing constructs and models based on earlier UML versions. For ongoing projects the advantages (more exact modeling) have to be weighed against the disadvantages (additional work).

3

Modeling Business Systems

Commercial IT systems are used mainly for dealing with business transactions of various sorts. Because of this, the development and integration of IT systems determine the views of those business processes that are embedded in the IT system. The business system model and its business processes serve as the basis for this. In this chapter we will discuss the construction of business system models.

To ensure smooth business transactions through the use of IT systems, it is indispensable to know and understand the **business environment** of IT systems. Therefore, analysis and modeling of business processes are important components of development and integration of IT systems.

Today, most IT systems are not only embedded in a business environment, but are also connected with other IT systems. Thus, every new IT system has to fit not into one, but two different target environments:

- **Integration on the business-process level**: Each IT system has to be assigned the activities of a business process in a way that enables correct and efficient execution of the entire business process with all involved components.

- **Integration at the IT-system level**: Communication with other IT systems involved in the business process has to go smoothly. This requires semantically and technically perfect interfaces. Integration on the IT-system level will be discussed in Chapter 5, *Modeling for System Integration*.

Answer the following questions for yourself:

- When was the last time you experienced a functional gap between a new IT system and its environment that appeared during the development process?
- How many IT systems do you know that do not optimally support, or even obstruct, the operating processes of users?
- When was the last time you experienced an IT system having to be halted on the day it was rolled out, because a functional error in the interfaces made operation impossible?

We don't want to look only at the dynamic aspects of our model, but also at the static elements. Because of this, we will construct a business system model that entails both business processes and business structures.

3.1 Business Processes and Business Systems

3.1.1 What is a Business Process?

Most people intuitively understand a **business process** to be a *procedure* or *event* with the purpose of reaching a *goal*. When looking at our UML Airport we can find many different business processes and goals:

- The goal of our passenger is to go on vacation. To achieve this goal, he has to book a flight and hotel, pack his bags, drive to the UML Airport, check in and board his airplane, exit the plane at his destination airport, go to the hotel, move into his room, and unpack his bags.

- The owner of the newsstand at the UML Airport wants to sell her goods. For this, she buys items inexpensively and sells them to her customers at a higher price.

- In order for passengers to check in at the UML Airport, an employee of passenger services accepts their tickets and luggage, inquires about their seat preferences, and uses an IT system. By the end of the procedure, the passengers receive their boarding passes on which their reserved seats and the appropriate gates are marked.

As you can see, business processes are often completed in several steps. These steps are also referred to as **activities**, and have to be completed in a predetermined order. The newsstand owner cannot sell any goods unless she has purchased them beforehand.

A passenger packs his or her suitcase before he or she drives to the airport. The employee of passenger services at the check-in counter can only issue a boarding pass after check-in is completed (Figure 3.1):

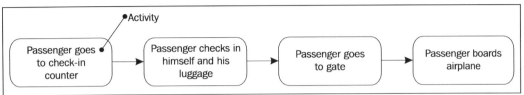

Figure 3.1 Activity of the business process "Passenger Services" (simplified)

Activities can run *sequentially* or in *parallel*. Thus, a passenger can buy a bottle of whiskey in the duty-free shop, while his or her luggage is being loaded into the Airbus 320 to London.

Individual activities can be organizationally **distributed**. The check-in procedure takes place at the check-in counter and is performed by an employee of passenger services, while the subsequent boarding occurs at a different location and is performed by different employees of passenger services.

Usually, the activities of a business process are interdependent. This interdependency is created by the interaction of all the activities belonging to a business process that pursue one common goal.

Think about which of the following activities are not interdependent with our case study, because they do not pursue the goal of our passenger to go on vacation in an Airbus 320:

- Loading of the Airbus 320 with food and beverages
- Fueling of a Boeing 737
- Cleaning of the UML Airport restrooms
- Promotion of a UML Airport employee to vice-president

3.1.2 Definition of the Workflow Management Coalition

Official definitions of the terms **process** and **business process** were adopted by the **Workflow Management Coalition**. The following definitions can be found in the glossary of the **Workflow Reference Model** of the Workflow Management Coalition (*The Work Flow Reference Model*, February 1999: http://www.wfmc.org):

"A process is a coordinated (parallel and/or serial) set of process activity(s) that are connected in order to achieve a common goal. Such activities may consist of manual activity(s) and/or workflow activity(s)."

According to this definition, a process is a set of activities that occur in a coordinated manner, either in parallel or one after another, and that pursue one common goal. These activities can be performed manually or when supported by an IT system.

"A business process is a kind of process in the domain of business organizational structure and policy for the purpose of achieving business objectives."

3.1.3 Business Systems

So far, we have explained business processes. Business processes are dynamic in nature and involve activities. However, if we want to look at the entire business system, we also have to consider the static aspects. This involves, for instance, the organizational structures within which business processes are conducted. This also involves various business objects and information objects, such as tickets or orders. For the static and dynamic aspects as a whole, we use the term business system.

In business terminology, a **business system** refers to the value-added chain, which describes the value-added process, meaning the supply of goods and services. A business can span one or several business systems.

Each business system, in itself, generates economic benefit. Thus, the business administrative meaning of business system does not differ very much from our use of the term business system. We also refer to the 'results' of a business system as 'functionality'.

For the analysis and modeling of a business system it is important to define system limits. A business system that is to be modeled can span an entire organization. In this case, we talk about an **organization model**.

It is also possible to consider and model only a selected part of an organization. In our case study, an IT system is to be integrated into the Passenger Services operation. Therefore, it is sufficient to observe this operation and to narrow the business system to Passenger Services only.

Passenger Services is a division within the UML Airport, with employees, organizational structure, an IT system, and defined tasks (Figure 3.2). The surrounding divisions, such as baggage transportation or catering, also belong to the UML Airport, but not to our business system. So, we will treat them like other, external, business systems:

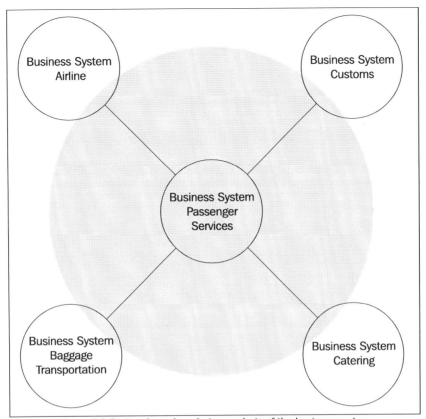

Figure 3.2 System boundary during analysis of the business system

We are not interested in any of the external business systems as a whole, but only in the *interfaces* between them and our business system. For instance, the staff of passenger services need to know that they have to transfer passengers' luggage to baggage transportation, so that it can be loaded into the airplane. Of course, for this, passenger services have to know *how* baggage transportation accepts luggage, so that it can be made available accordingly. It is possible that the IT systems of passenger services and baggage transportation will have to be connected, meaning that interfaces will have to be created. On the other hand, passenger services are completely unconcerned with how baggage transportation is organized, and whether each suitcase is individually carried across the runway or carts are used to transport luggage to the airplane.

3.1.4 Using UML to Model Business Processes and Business Systems

Before we move on to the modeling of business processes and business systems with UML, we should ask ourselves whether UML is even suitable for the modeling of business processes and business systems. For this purpose we will take a look at UML's definition by OMG (Object Management Group Inc.—the international association that promotes open standards for object-oriented applications, which publishes each version of UML that is submitted for standardization at http://www.omg.org):

> "The Unified Modeling Language is a visual language for specifying, constructing, and documenting the artifacts of systems"—*UML Unified Modeling Language: Infrastructure, Version 2.0, Final Adopted Specifications*, September 2003.

This definition indicates that UML is a language for the modeling and representation of systems in general, and thus, also of business systems.

In any case, UML fulfills at least one of the requirements of business-system modeling: it reflects various views of a business system, in order to capture its different aspects. The various standardized diagram types of UML meet this requirement, because every diagram gives a different view of the modeled business system.

We reach the limits of UML when modeling extensive business process projects, for instance, business process reengineering, or when modeling entire organizations. However, for these kinds of projects powerful methods and tools are available, such as **Architecture of Integrated IT Systems (ARIS)**. This doesn't mean that we want to keep anyone from using UML for projects like that, although we recommend a thorough study of the UML specifications (*OMG*: *Unified Modeling Language*: *Superstructure, Version 2.0, Revised Final Adopted Specification*, October 2004) and the use of CASE tools.

This text is tailored toward projects with the goal of developing IT systems. Moreover, it is tailored toward projects for which a concern of the business system is the assurance of the smooth integration of an IT system. The following characteristics mark such projects:

- Those business processes that are affected by the construction and integration of IT systems are considered.

- Business-process modeling is not the focus of these projects. Instead, the model serves as the foundation for the construction and integration of IT systems. Business process integration can determine the success or failure of such a project; but the main task still is the construction of IT systems.

- Because budgets are often tight, time investment in the methodology and language required for business-process modeling should not amount to more than 5–10% of the total project effort.

3.1.5 Practical Tips for Modeling Business Processes

Often one is warned about the complexity of business process analysis and business-process modeling. However, in our experience most business processes are thoroughly understandable and controllable. Rather, the lack of clarity and transparency makes them seem more complex than they really are.

In many cases, existing business processes are documented poorly or not at all. This can be traced to the fact that for many years most functionalities were treated as 'islands' instead of parts of comprehensive business processes. Because of that, the link between activities—the process chain—is missing. If this overview is missing, business processes seem complicated.

There are more hurdles to overcome if business processes are handled by IT systems. Most of the time, documentation of the manual workflow that is carried out between individual systems is not available. In other cases, the functionality of IT systems is unknown because processes run automatically, hidden somewhere in a black box, and only the input and output are visible.

Existing business process architectures or reference models that already exist can speed up and ease the modeling process. Comparing processes with similar or identical processes in other organizations can be helpful in identifying discrepancies and deriving possibilities for improvement.

3.2 One Model—Two Views

A business system can be viewed from different perspectives. Because of this, our business system model consists of two different views. Each of the views emphasizes certain aspects of the business system, and each of them is linked to the other. We clarify the different views in Figure 3.3.

Viewing a business system from the outside, we take on the role of a customer, a business partner, a supplier, or another business system. From this **external view**, only those business processes that involve outsiders are of interest. The external view describes the environment of a business system. The business system itself remains a black box.

Within the business system, we find *employees* and *tools* that are responsible for fulfilling the demands of the environment, and for handling the necessary business processes. Behind the business processes are *workflows* and *IT systems*. Each individual employee is part of the *organizational structure*. Normally this **internal view** remains hidden to outsiders.

Take a look at our case study:

- Think about what services Passenger Services provides to you, as a passenger.
- Which employees of Passenger Services are you in contact with as a passenger?
- As a passenger, do you see the procedures that a check-in employee performs, when you are issued your boarding pass? Would you like to know how your luggage ends up in the airplane, or do you not care, as long it doesn't get lost?

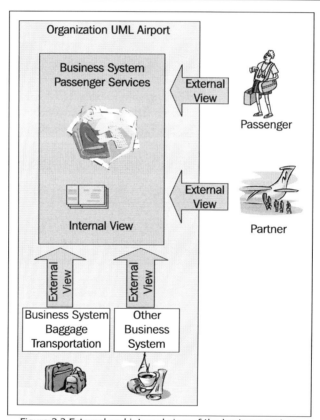

Figure 3.3 External and internal view of the business system

We begin with the external view in modeling our business system. In this way, we start with the description of the business system from the perspective of customers, business partners, and suppliers:

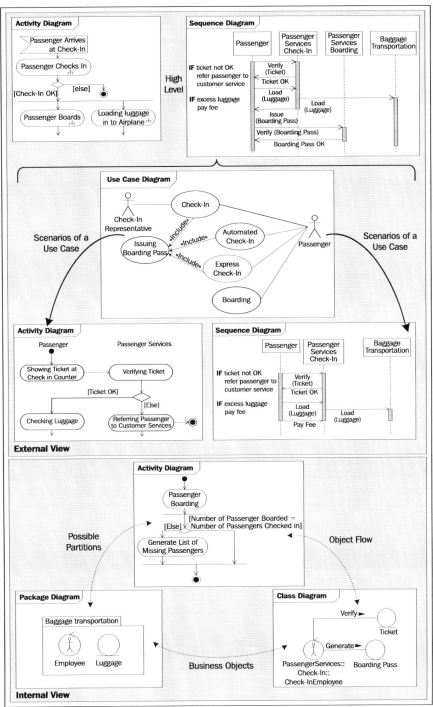

Figure 3.4 The different views and diagrams

Following this, the internal view describes *how* the business system provides these services. The use cases of the external view serve well as the basis for constructing test scenarios, which are necessary for testing a finished IT system.

The individual views that we use for the business-system model, and the UML diagrams that they incorporate, are depicted in Figure 3.4.

3.3 External View

3.3.1 What Benefit does a Business System Provide?

As a customer or business partner of an organization, you don't care if transactions within an organization take place manually or are IT-based. You are also not interested in how many forms employees of the organization have to fill out, whether it is 2 or 20. Customers and business partners are merely interested in what kind of goods and services can be offered, and how they can make use of them. The customer view describes the interactions with external parties, such as customers and partners, and presents the business system as a black box.

> Consider a business system, such as passenger services or an airport newsstand from the outside. Which output is of interest for customers and business partners? Is the output a service or material goods?

From the business administrative view, the goal of a business system is (profitable) output (also see Section 3.1.3, *Business Systems*). Output can generally be divided into goods and services. The production of goods could be, for example, the production of boxes of the finest Swiss chocolates.

But how do we distinguish services? Services are intangible goods, such as reserving a seat or loading luggage into an airplane. Unlike material goods, services can't be rendered unless suppliers and customers make contact. However, a service can involve material goods. If a box of Swiss chocolates is sold at our newsstand, this transaction is a service. We can see from this example that the transaction of material goods is treated as a service because it involves a customer.

Consequently, the supply of material goods and services is relevant for the external view. The external view does not describe how employees and IT systems provide goods and services, and how business processes are transacted within the business system. In the external view, only those activities that involve outsiders are of concern.

In our case study, it is important for a passenger to know that he or she can check in with a valid ticket at the check-in counter, and that he or she will subsequently receive a boarding pass. What employees and IT systems actually have to do in order for him or her to receive a boarding pass remains hidden from the passenger—and in most cases he or she does not want to know, anyway.

In practice, we have observed that the external view is difficult to represent, if the employees of an organization, who are located *within* the business system, develop the model. It is difficult for a person within a business system, who knows all the internal transactions, to reconstruct the view of the customer, which does not consider internal transactions at all. If external and internal views are mixed, they inhibit the clear view from the outside of a business system and its business processes. (Thus, user-unfriendly systems are created!) Therefore, consult unbiased staff members, who can put themselves in the outsider's place more easily, for instance, employees of other divisions or external consultants.

Business Use Cases

Before we converge to the **business use cases**, we would like to take a look at the general definition of a use case in UML. A use case is the specification of a set of actions performed by a system, which yields an observable result that is typically of value for one or more actors or other stakeholders of the system (OMG: *Unified Modeling Language: Superstructure, Version 2.0, Revised Final Adopted Specification, October 2004*).

What is an observable, valuable result in a business system? This question—how to find use cases—has preoccupied analysts and designers since the first day the term was used. The use cases of our business system are the services of a business system that are offered to customers, business partners, or other business systems. In contrast to this, the functionality that exists within a business system, which is neither visible nor accessible to outsiders, represents an internal activity, meaning an internal business process.

On the level of the business model we use the term business use case instead of use case. The reason behind this differentiation is a clear separation and the elimination of mix-ups in the transition from the business system model to the IT system model. The business use case is reserved to the business system model. Beyond this, there are no differences between a business use case and a use case.

Business processes can be performed manually or be IT-assisted. Nowadays, entire business processes can be initiated and conducted completely without human help. Corresponding to this reality, business use cases can comprise manual tasks, as well as IT-assisted activities.

If we look at our Hanseatic merchant's trading office, we find exclusively business use cases that are conducted manually. If a customer of the trading office orders Russian fur, the clerk uses pen and ink to enter the order into the order book. Thus, business use cases already existed in medieval times.

In our case study, manually conducted passenger services as well IT-assisted activities are performed. For example, the IT system of passenger services performs seat reservations for passengers, while an employee conducts the verification of the ticket manually.

A passenger who checks in at a machine does not even encounter a human being. The check-in machine performs the entire business use case.

Actors

Outside of the business system are, for instance, customers or business partners, who use the output of the business system under consideration. It's not necessary that these **outsiders** know in detail how a business case is conducted. For our passengers, it is important to know that they can buy a bottle of whiskey in the duty-free shop. The bottle of whiskey is a *material good* that the duty-free shop provides; selling the bottle to the customer, on the other hand, is a *service*. The passenger does not care how the duty-free shop employee conducts the sale. These outsiders are called **actors** (see Figure 3.5):

Figure 3.5 Outsiders and staff members

A business use case is always initiated by an actor, meaning that a customer or business partner utilizes a service. Our passenger, who strolls through the duty-free shop, considers a Scottish Malt Whisky a cheap bargain, and decides to buy a bottle. This makes him the initiator of the sale. During the transaction of a business use case, actors are able to interact with the humans and IT systems within the business system that are responsible for the transaction. For example, our passenger has to hand over a certain amount of money, in order to receive the bottle of whiskey.

Activities that are initiated by employees or IT system within the business system are not business use cases of the external view, but are activities of the internal view and will be represented in the activity diagram or sequence diagram of the internal view.

As you can see, the actors of business systems can be humans, organizations, or IT systems. Even if organizations are represented as actors, as in the case of baggage transportation, we ultimately find people or IT systems behind the actors that initiate and handle cases. However, what are relevant for our models are the **roles** that are played. On the level of the business system model, it is not important if it is a person, an IT system, an organization, or a division of an organization, a machine, or any other system that takes up a certain role.

Take another look at our case study and try to locate all persons, organization units, and IT systems involved. Then, try to structure them according to the following criteria:

- Which is an outsider (customer, business partner, etc.) and what output does this outsider use?
- What persons are located within passenger services as employees, and what tasks do they perform?
- Which IT systems are involved?
- In order for a passenger to buy a bottle of whiskey duty-free, an employee of the duty-free shop has to check the boarding pass of the passenger, accept money, pack the bottle in a bag, and hand out a receipt. Which of these activities belong to the internal view, and which belong to the external view?

3.3.2 The Elements of a View

The following types of UML diagrams represent the external view:

- **Use case diagrams** show actors, business use cases, and their relationships. Use case diagrams do not describe procedures. Alternative scenarios also remain hidden. These diagrams give a good overview of the functionality of a business system.

- **Activity diagrams** describe procedures, in our case, the business processes of the business system. The subjects of these descriptions are interactions between actors and the business system, meaning the goods and services that are offered to customers and business partners. On the basis of activity diagrams, outsiders can identify how to interact with the business system. They are especially useful to illustrate sequences, alternatives, and parallel events. Activity diagrams can be created in various degrees of detail.

- **Sequence diagrams** show the chronological chain of interactions. They do not depict every event with all its branches and parallelisms, but the information that is exchanged between the involved parties.
  These diagrams are a good basis for data and information exchange with partners and customers (Figure 3.6):

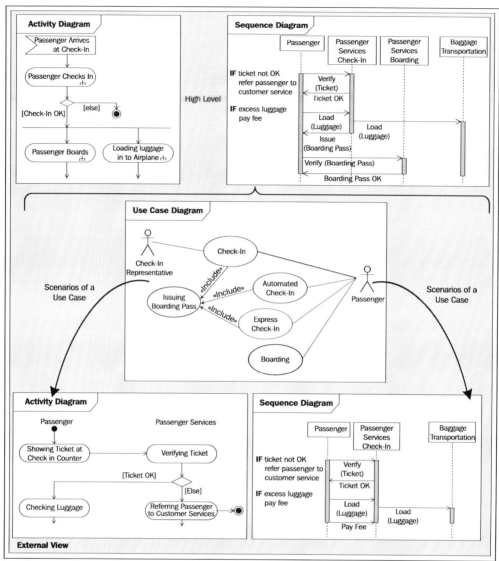

Figure 3.6 The external view

UML diagrams for the description of business use cases can be annotated with written descriptions and illustrative figures. Not every diagram has to be used in each case. Which diagram type should be used depends on which system characteristics need to be emphasized. In any case, we recommend creating use case diagrams, because this diagram type is well suited for communicating with system partners and domain experts about the basic functionality and the context of the system. High-level activity diagrams with a low degree of detail, which can include several use cases, are also well suited for this purpose.

When refining business use cases and identifying the various scenarios, it becomes necessary to describe the various activities with activity diagrams.

Sequence diagrams show the information exchange with partners and customers (see Chapter 5, *Modeling for System Integration*). In our practical experience, sequence diagrams meet great acceptance in the field of business-process modeling. This is because they are easy to read and require only a few graphical elements. As long as some basic knowledge exists about the technical events, sequence diagrams are often more appropriate for an overview of the interactions of a business system than activity diagrams.

3.3.3 Use Case Diagrams

Use case diagrams show business use cases, actors, and the relationships between them. The relationships between actors and business use cases state that an actor can use a certain functionality of the business system. You will not find any information about how or in what chronological sequence these services are rendered (Figure 3.7):

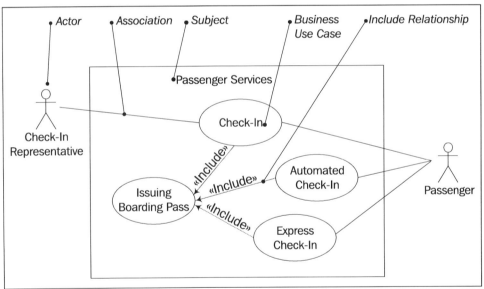

Figure 3.7 The elements of the use case diagram

We use the following elements in use case diagrams:

Actor: An actor represents a role that an outsider takes on when interacting with the business system. For instance, an actor can be a customer, a business partner, a supplier, or another business system.

Every actor has a name:

Instead of a stick figure, other symbols can be used as well, if they fit the characteristics of the actor and lead to practical, easy-to-read diagrams.

Association: An association is the relationship between an actor and a business use case. It indicates that an actor can use a certain functionality of the business system—the business use case:

Unfortunately, the association does not give any information about the way in which the functionality is used. If a business use case includes several actors, it is not apparent in the use case diagram if each actor can conduct the business use case alone, or if the actors conduct the business use case together. In fact, association only means that an actor is *involved* in the business use case.

Business Use Case: A business use case describes the interaction between an actor and a business system, meaning it describes the functionality of the business system that the actor utilizes:

A business use case is described from the actor's perspective. Apart from the special use of the business use case as a use case within a business system, there is no difference between the business use case and a 'normal' use case.

Include Relationship: The include relationship is a relationship between two business use cases that signifies that the business use case on the side to which the arrow points is included in the use case on the other side of the arrow. This means that for one functionality that the business system provides, another functionality of the business system is accessed.

In this way, functionalities that are accessed repeatedly can be depicted as individual business use cases, which can be used in multiple ways:

At times, the direction of the arrow can be confusing; the relationship has to be read alongside the direction of the arrow (check-in includes issuing the boarding pass).

Subject: A subject describes a business system that has one or more business use cases attached to it. A subject is represented by a rectangle that surrounds attached business use cases and is tagged with a name:

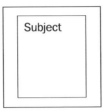

Depicting the subject (and with it the system limits) is optional.

Reading Use Case Diagrams

Figure 3.8 illustrates a use case diagram with the actors: the **passenger** (1) and the **check-in representative** (2), as well as the business use cases **check-in** (3) and **express check-in** (4):

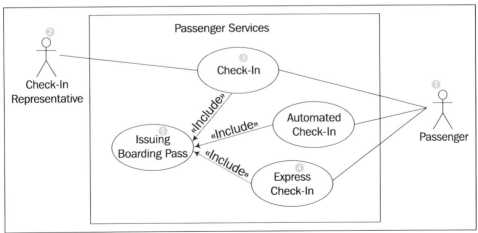

Figure 3.8 Use case diagram

Depending on what you are interested in, you would begin reading with an actor or with a business use case. Starting with the actor, **passenger** (1), we find the associations (lines) to the two business use cases, **check-in** (3) and **express check-in** (4). This means that people, who appear as passengers, can either go through check-in, or express check-in, which can be conducted without luggage.

That one of the two business use cases is below the other means nothing. A use case diagram does *not* document a meaningful order in which business use cases could be conducted. Of course, the order matters for the description and linking of business processes. This aspect is pictured in activity diagrams (see Section 3.3.5 *Activity Diagrams*).

The actor **check-in representative** (2) also has an association to the business use case **check-in** (3). This means that not only the passenger, but also someone who represents him or her can check in. That the actor, **passenger** (1), also has an association to the use case **check-in** (3) means that the passenger and the check-in representative can both check-in. However, what the diagram does not show clearly is that it *does not* mean that they perform the check-in together. This fact can only be described in another diagram (see Section 3.3.5, *Activity Diagrams*) or in the form of a comment that can contain informal text.

That the actor **check-in representative** (2) only has an association to the business use case **check-in** (3) means that at the UML Airport a representative of the passenger cannot perform an **express check-in** (4).

You can see that such a simple diagram can contain quite a lot of information. The business use case **check-in** (3) and the business use case **express check-in** (4) each have an include relationship with **issuing boarding pass** (5). Both use the business use case issuing boarding pass at some point in their own interaction. (Use cases cannot define *when* another use case is executed.) Sometime during check-in the boarding pass is issued and handed to the passenger or check-in representative. Figure 3.9 attempts to clarify this procedure once more:

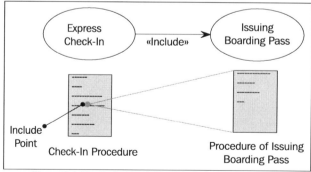

Figure 3.9 The include relationship between use cases

3.3.4 Constructing Use Case Diagrams

The following checklist shows the steps necessary for the construction of use case diagrams. After this, we will explain the individual steps further.

Checklist 3.1 Constructing Use Case Diagrams from the External View:

- Collect information sources—How am I supposed to know that?
- Identify potential actors—Which partners and customers use the goods and services of the business system?
- Identify potential business use cases—Which goods and services can actors draw upon?
- Connect business use cases—Who can make use of what goods and services of the business system?
- Describe actors—Who or what do the actors represent?
- Search for more business use cases—What else needs to be done?
- Edit business use cases—What actually has to be included in a business use case?
- Document business use cases—What happens in a business use case?
- Model relationships between business use cases—What activities are conducted repeatedly?
- Verify the view—Is everything correct?

We deliberately chose the order in which the steps are performed. However, this order is not mandatory, since in practice, the individual steps often overlap heavily.

On one hand, a general understanding of the business system and business processes is important for the realization of each individual step. On the other hand, for many steps it is also necessary to consult knowledge carriers. It makes little sense to cling to the personal view of the analyst, who knows too little about the area of application.

Collecting Information Sources—How am I Supposed to Know That?

As a first step, it is important to find knowledge carriers, in order for analysts and knowledge carriers to work out the basic principles together. Such knowledge carriers are, for example:

- People who are involved in performing, operating, and controlling business processes
- Users of similar or related IT systems
- Customers, who are often critical and creative knowledge carriers
- Business partners
- Domain experts
- Management
- External observers

Several helpful techniques have proven to be practical for the analysis and understanding of business processes:

- Observing employees at work
- Participating in the business processes being investigated
- Taking the role of an outsider (e.g., of a customer)
- Giving out surveys
- Performing interviews
- Brainstorming with everyone involved
- Discussing with domain experts
- Reviewing existing forms, documentation, specifications, handbooks, and work tools
- Describing organizational structure and workflow management
- Reviewing organization charts and job descriptions

- Read through the introduction to the case study in Chapter 2, *Basic Principles and Background* once more. In this introduction, we explain the basics of the case study, to help with understanding its business processes.
- In your mind, run through all the roles that you can think of and their business processes (passenger, clerk in the duty-free shop, etc.).
- Which activities can you think of from the view of the passenger? How would you try to freshen up your memory?

The result of this first step is often a collection of forms, work instructions, completed surveys, existing process descriptions, business objects such as tickets or boarding passes, etc. This overview is often not yet complete, and will be further extended during the modeling process.

Identifying Potential Actors—Which Partners and Customers Use the Goods and Services of the Business System?

This step is all about identifying potential actors. Here, this rule applies: the more the merrier. You can work with these actors in later steps; or they can be reduced in number or combined.

More potential actors can be found by answering the following questions (e.g., through consulting knowledge carriers). In doing this, it is advisable to create groups of people and types of organizations by abstracting directly from concrete examples of specific persons and organizations:

- Which customers are customers of the business system, and which are customers of the business processes?

- Who are the external partners of the business system? Which goods and services do these external partners use?

- Which in-house positions and organization units are partners of the business system and use its goods and services?

- With what external business systems does the business system interact?

As a first step, the previous explanations of our case study result in the following actors:

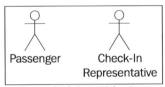

Figure 3.10 Potential actors

In addition to the passenger, who represents travelers, there is the check-in representative. The **check-in representative** is a person who is not the actual passenger, but an agent of the passenger. The check-in representative has the task of performing the check-in with the ticket of the passenger.

Identifying Potential Business Use Cases—Which Goods and Services can Actors Draw Upon?

This step is about finding potential business use cases. The rule—the more the merrier—applies here as well (in reasonable moderation). Potential business use cases can be found by answering the following questions:

- Which goods or services are provided to and used by the customer?

- Which goods or services are provided to and used by external partners?

- Which goods and services that are provided by the business system involve suppliers (suppliers of goods and suppliers of services)?

- What are the individual actors doing?

- How and on what occasions does communication take place with other business systems or business partners?

- Which events trigger what activities?

First considerations of our case study result in the following business use cases:

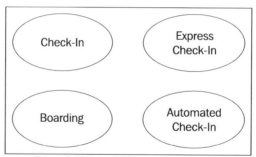

Figure 3.11 Potential business use cases

Initially, the business use cases can only be described in a concise and informal manner:

- The **check-in** procedure includes submitting the ticket, baggage check-in, seat reservation, and issuing and handing over the boarding pass.

- Passengers who only have hand luggage can use **express check-in**. No baggage check-in is performed.

- During **boarding**, the boarding pass of the passenger is verified at the gate.

- **Automated check-in** is conducted without the help of a check-in clerk, directly at a machine (screen). Baggage cannot be checked in.

Practical Tips

For us, in practice, the observation technique has proven effective for identifying business use cases. By observing people involved in the business processes, activity lists can be created. Following this, the activities can be grouped by events that lead to the first business use cases.

Connecting Business Use Cases—Who Can Make Use of What Goods and Services of the Business System?

By assigning business use cases to actors, a first draft of the use case diagram evolves (Figure 3.12). This is achieved by answering the following question:

- Which customers or business partners have what functionalities available to them?

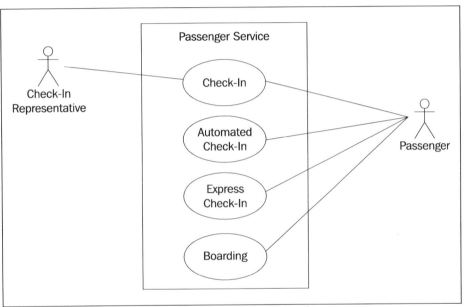

Figure 3.12 First draft of the use case diagram

With this first draft we obtain the basis from which we can further edit and refine the use case diagram.

The passenger can choose between a normal check-in, automated check-in, and express check-in. The passenger walks to the gate and presents his or her boarding pass. The check-in representative can perform a regular check-in, but is not able to perform express check-in and automated check-in.

Describing Actors—Who or What do the Actors Represent?

An actor in a diagram has to be named in a way that clarifies the role that is represented. Here, it is of utter importance that the terminology of the domain area, meaning a business-oriented term, is used. In addition to the name, an actor can be further defined with a description. The question to this end is:

- How can an actor be described further? For instance, this description can include an area of responsibility, requirements from the system, or a formal definition of his, her, or its role. Don't be afraid to add job descriptions or organizational profiles (for example of a catering company)—even if these are not represented in UML.

Searching for More Business Use Cases—What else Needs to be Done?

Once you have found several business use cases, they can be used as starting points for further questions. Starting from a particular business use case, the following questions can be asked:

- Is there anything that has to be done at some point beforehand, prior to accessing a particular functionality?

- Is there anything that has to be done at some point afterwards, after performing a particular business use case?

- Is there anything that needs to be done if nobody performs a particular business use case?

In doing so, it is important to consider the proper business system. Many of the events that occur before or after a business use case take place outside the business system under consideration. In our case study, for instance, booking the flight or getting to the airport does not belong to the system being considered.

If we take a closer look, we notice that a passenger often travels with luggage, which he or she checks in. Baggage transportation is responsible for loading luggage into the airplane. Baggage transportation is carried out by an independent organization, known as a handling agent. Consequently, it is considered an actor, more specifically, an outside service provider. It does not matter for our diagram that individual employees of the partner enterprise perform these tasks.

Ten minutes before a flight leaves, baggage transportation requests a passenger list from passenger services, which includes every passenger who checked in, but did not board the airplane. On the basis of this list all affected luggage will be unloaded again from the airplane. If the flight is an international flight, the customs authorities of the country in which the destination airport is located also request a passenger list.

This results in two new actors: baggage transportation and the customs authorities at the destination airport (Figure 3.13):

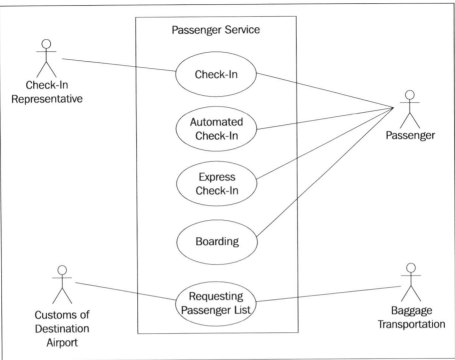

Figure 3.13 Extended use case diagram

Editing Business Use Cases—What actually has to be Included in a Business Use Case?

Without a doubt, it is difficult to find the right amount of detail in the modeling of business systems. If almost all the activities of an actor in a business use case are combined, the use case diagram will lose practically all of its significance. If the activities are itemized too thoroughly, the use case diagram gets too complex and contains too many activities with interrelationships that are hardly recognizable.

Fortunately, some criteria will help you determine the optimal scope of a business use case. For this purpose, ask yourself the following questions:

- Does the business use case consist of a behaviourally related sequence of interactions that belong together (an interaction sequence)?

Items that are included in a business use case have to be directly related. Issuing a boarding pass and searching for lost luggage are not related at all. Business use cases that violate this criterion have to be divided. This prevents the occurrence of oversized business use cases.

- How many actors are involved in a business use case? Business use cases that have too many actors have to be divided. This also prevents oversized business use cases.

- Does the business use case deliver tangible and relevant goods or services? A business use case is not supposed to describe incomplete steps, for example, counting pieces of luggage. Rather, at least in a regular case, it is supposed to produce a benefit that has meaning from a customer's perspective. Business use cases that violate this criterion have to be combined with other business use cases. This way, undersized business use cases are prevented.

- Is the business use case never performed alone, but always in a sequence in combination with other business use cases? A business use case is not supposed to describe goods and services that are only used in combination with other goods and services. Business use cases that violate this criterion, have to be combined with other business use cases. This also prevents undersized business use cases.

- Is the business use case initiated by an actor? Business use cases that are not initiated by an actor are not use cases but internal activities that are depicted in the internal view of the business system.

A review of the existing business use cases on the basis of these questions can lead to the consolidation or division of business use cases.

Documenting Business Use Cases—What Happens in a Business Use Case?

To understand a business use case, the information from the use case diagram is not sufficient. The chain of interactions and of the various scenarios that are behind each business use case have to be described. This means that the goods and services that the business system provides have to be described, namely the chain of events from the perspective of the customer or business partner.

In addition to purely verbal description, documentation in activity diagrams and sequence diagrams has proven to be especially valuable. The construction of these diagram types will be treated in the following sections: 3.3.5, *Activity Diagrams*, and 3.3.9, *High-Level Sequence Diagrams*.

Modeling Relationships between Business Use Cases—What Activities are Conducted Repeatedly?

If you realize that certain parts of an interaction are the same in several business use cases, you can extract these similarities and combine them into their own business use case. This new business use case can be used in other business use cases with an **include relationship**.

In our case study, the business use case **issuing boarding pass** has not yet been assigned. We know that the boarding pass is generated and issued during check-in. At some point during the business use cases check-in, express check-in, and automated check-in, the boarding pass is issued (see Figure 3.14):

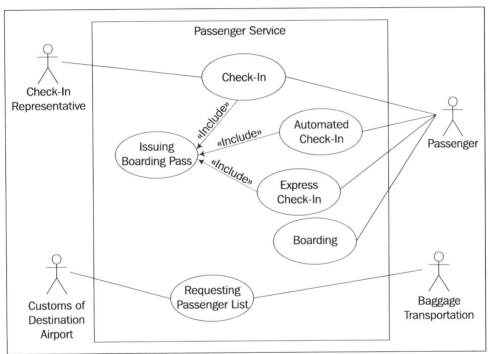

Figure 3.14 Extended use case diagram

Verifying the View—Is Everything Correct?

All diagrams and records have to be verified by the knowledge carriers. What we should ask the knowledge carriers for every diagram or view is:

- Is everything that is contained in the diagram correct and complete?

Even if knowledge carriers can read and understand diagrams themselves (they can use the reading directions in this text), we should still read the diagrams to them. Only with this last step is the circle completed. This results in a verified view, which reflects a current shared understanding of business systems and business processes.

The completed use case diagram can be verified with the following checklist:

Checklist 3.2 Verifying Use Case Diagrams from the External View:

- **Completeness**: The use case diagram is complete if there are no further business use cases in the system. All goods and services that are available to customers and partners of the business system are depicted in the form of business use cases (if necessary, business use cases can be spread out into several diagrams).
- **Extent**: All business use cases that are included in the use case diagram are real business use cases, meaning they meet the definition of a business use case.
- **Degree of detail**: The degree of detail of the business use cases meets the following requirements:
  A business use case represents a behaviorally coherent interaction sequence.

  A business use case is initiated by an actor, and has only a few actors.

  A business use case represents a functionality that is tangible and that yields a relevant result.
- **Relationships between business use cases**: Include relationships are applied properly.
- **Naming and describing**: The names of business use cases describe the functionalities that the business system provides. The naming was done in accordance with the normal terminology of the business system.
- **Actors**: The actors in the use case diagram represent roles taken up by outside persons, organizations, or other business systems during interactions.

Practical Tips

When using use case diagrams for modeling business systems and business processes, it is advisable to keep the level of abstraction low. For the comprehensibility of the diagrams and for communication between the involved parties, it is better to add redundancies than to abstract too much.

It is of fundamental importance that the terminology of the business processes or the organization is used, and that the descriptions of the business use cases are chosen in a way that can be understood intuitively.

Terminology from the field of **Information Technology (IT)** does not belong in use case diagrams on the business-process level. The mixing of terms from the business process and IT communities leads to poor results. In reality, we often encounter use cases that are already very close to IT on the business-process level, e.g., updating a customer index. This leads to confusion in two aspects:

- Users—meaning people who are involved in business processes, and who are not familiar with IT terminology—do not understand the business use cases. Since business use cases describe the performance requirements for a business system, the business system and business processes cannot be understood, and therefore cannot be verified. In a project with poorly formulated business use cases, an IT department presented the business use cases to users for verification and received just one short answer: "Men throwing arrows?!".

- Technical details on the level of business use cases distract from the business-process specific requirements for a system.

3.3.5 Activity Diagrams

Activity diagrams, which are related to program flow plans (flowcharts), are used to illustrate activities. In the external view, we use activity diagrams for the description of those business processes that describe the functionality of the business system.

Contrary to use case diagrams, in activity diagrams it is obvious whether actors can perform business use cases together or independently from one another.

Activity diagrams allow you to think functionally. Purists of the object-oriented approach probably dislike this fact. We, on the other hand, regard this fact as a great advantage, since users of object-oriented methods, as well as users of functional thinking patterns, find a common and familiar display format, which is a significant aid for business-process modeling.

Because it is possible to explicitly describe parallel events, the activity diagram is well suited for the illustration of business processes, since business processes rarely occur in a linear manner and often exhibit parallelisms.

Activity diagrams can be developed in various degrees of detail. They can be refined step by step. In the external view, activity diagrams, just like use case diagrams, exclusively represent business processes and activities from the outside perspective. Refining diagrams does not mean describing process details that are performed within the business system, which often leads to an unnoticed shift to the internal view (Figure 3.15):

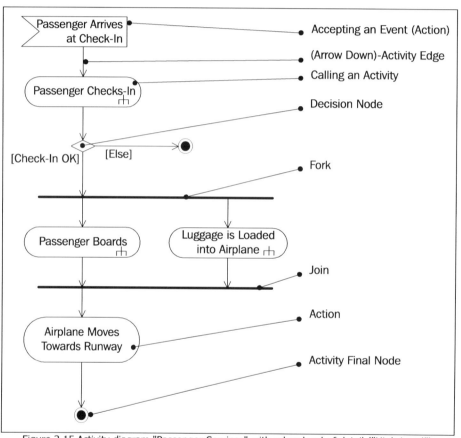

Figure 3.15 Activity diagram "Passenger Services" with a low level of detail ("High Level")

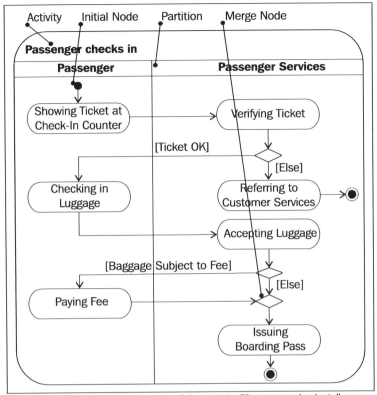

Figure 3.16 Activity diagram of the activity "Passenger checks in"

Activity: An activity diagram illustrates one individual activity. In our context, an activity represents a business process (Figure 3.16). Fundamental elements of the activity are actions and control elements (decision, division, merge, initiation, end, etc.):

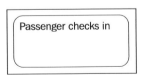

Elements are connected by so-called "activity edges" and form the "control flow", which can also be casually called 'flow'. The execution of an activity can contain parallel flows. A border can surround the activity, meaning the entire activity diagram.

Action: An action is an individual step within an activity, for example, a calculation step that is not deconstructed any further. That does not necessarily mean that the action cannot be subdivided in the real world, but in this diagram will not be refined any further:

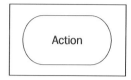

The action can possess input and output information The output of one action can be the input of a subsequent action within an activity. Specific actions are calling other actions, receiving an event, and sending signals.

Calling an Activity (Action): With this symbol an activity can be called from within another activity. Calling, in itself, is an action; the outcome of the call is another activity:

In this way, activities can be nested within each other and can be represented with different levels of detail.

Accepting an Event (Action): This action waits for an event to occur. After the event is accepted, the flow that comes from this action (and is defined in the activity diagram) is executed. Accepting events is an important element for business processes in activity diagrams:

Many business processes are initiated by events, for example, processing an order by the receipt of an order, or delivery by the receipt of a payment.

Accepting a Time Event (Action): At a definite point in time, this action starts a flow in the activity diagram. An hourglass symbol can be used to represent the acceptance of a time event:

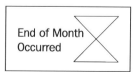

A typical example of a time event is triggering reminders after the deadline for payment has passed. We will discuss an example in Chapter 5, *Modeling for System Integration*.

Sending Signals (Action): Sending a signal means that a signal is being sent to an accepting activity:

The accepting activity accepts the signal with the action "accepting an event" and can react accordingly, meaning according to the flow that originates from this node in the activity diagram.

Edge (Control Flow): Edges, represented by arrows, connect the individual components of activity diagrams and illustrate the control flow of the activity:

Within the control flow an incoming arrow starts a single step of an activity; after the step is completed the flow continues along the outgoing arrow. A name can be attached to an edge (close to the arrow).

Decision Node: The diamond below represents a conditional branch point or decision node. A decision node has one input and two or more outputs:

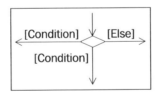

Each output has a condition attached to it, which is written in brackets. If a condition is met, the flow proceeds along the appropriate output. An 'else' output can be defined along which the flow can proceed if no other condition is met.

Merge Node: The diamond below has several inputs and only one output:

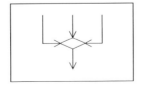

Its purpose is the merging of flows. The inputs are not synchronized; if a flow reaches such a node it proceeds at the output without waiting for the arrival of other flows.

Fork: For the branching of flows in two or more parallel flows we use a synchronization bar, which is depicted as a thick horizontal or vertical line:

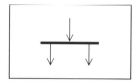

Branching allows parallel flows within activities. A fork has one input and two or more outputs.

Join: For the consolidation of two or more parallel flows we also use a synchronization bar, which is depicted as a thick horizontal or vertical line:

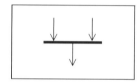

During consolidation synchronization takes place, meaning the flow proceeds only after *all* incoming flows have reached the consolidation point. Join has two or more inputs and one output.

Initial Node: The initial node is the starting point of an activity. An activity can have more than one initial node; in this case several flows start at the beginning of an activity:

It is also possible that an activity has no initial node, but is initiated by an event (action: accepting an event).

Activity Final Node: The activity final node indicates that an activity is completed. An activity diagram can have more than one exit in the form of activity final nodes:

If several parallel flows are present within an activity, all flows are stopped at the time the activity final node is reached.

Flow Final Node: A flow final node terminates a flow. Unlike the activity final node, which ends an entire activity, reaching a flow final node has no effect on other parallel flows that are being processed within the activity at the same point in time:

In this way, parallel flows can be terminated individually and selectively.

Activity Partition: The individual elements of an activity diagram can be divided into individual areas or 'partitions'. Various criteria can lead to the creation of these partitions: organization entities, cost centers, locations, etc:

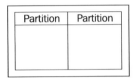

Individual steps of an activity will be assigned to these partitions. Each partition is set apart from its neighboring partition by a horizontal or vertical continuous line; from this stems the term **swimlanes**. Each partition receives a name. Partitions can be arranged in a two-dimensional manner; in this case the activity diagram is divided into individual cells like a grid.

Reading Activity Diagrams

You start reading at the **initial node**, or in Figure 3.17 with the acceptance of the event **passenger arrives at check-in** (1), and continue along the arrows of the control flow (2). The subsequent action **passenger checks in** (3) means that at this point the activity **'passenger checks in'** is processed. This is depicted in more detail in another activity diagram as is indicated by the 'fork' in the action symbol:

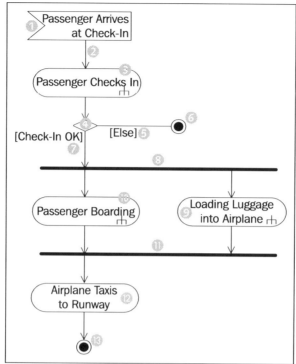

Figure 3.17 An activity diagram

If you follow the control flow, next you will come to a conditional branch or decision node (4): if the check-in is OK the next step along the control flow can follow. Otherwise (5), the passenger cannot fly and the task of passenger services is completed. This can be seen at the black dot with border—the activity final node.

After successful check-in (7) you come to a black cross bar. All arrows that come from this bar (7) symbolize flows that are processed simultaneously. While the luggage is being loaded onto the airplane (9) the passenger is boarding the airplane (10). Between point (8) and point (11) the flows are independent from one another. At the second cross bar (11) the simultaneously processed flows (9 and 10) are merged, meaning that only when the passenger is on the plane (10) *and* the luggage has been loaded onto the plane (9), does the control flow continue below the cross bar (11). In our example, one more action (12) and subsequent to that the final state (13) follow, meaning that after the passenger is on the plane (10) and the luggage has been loaded onto the plane (9), the airplane can taxi toward the runway (12). You can see here that the last action airplane taxis toward runway (12) is only defined as a single action, even though this process is very complex and could be described in many other activity diagrams. In our context, however, it is not important to describe this step in detail.

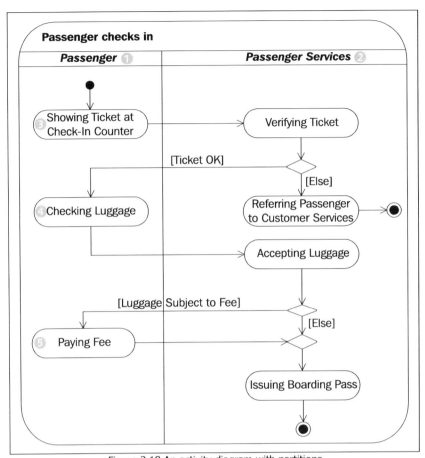

Figure 3.18 An activity diagram with partitions

The activity diagram in Figure 3.18 is divided into two partitions: **passenger** (1) and **passenger services** (2). The passenger, for instance, carries out **showing ticket at check-in counter** (3), **checking luggage** (4), and **paying fee** (5). All other actions are located in the partition (swimlane) of passenger services (2) and are carried out by passenger services.

3.3.6 Constructing Activity Diagrams

As always, we want to point out that the use of suitable terminology and appropriate naming of actions and activities are essential for the clarity and comprehensibility of activity diagrams. Do not despair if it takes hours to find appropriate names—in most cases the effort is worth it.

We recommend starting with activity diagrams that contain a low level of detail ('high level'), which can span several business use cases. This gives a good overview of the chain of interactions between customers and partners and the business system.

Later, in more detailed steps the scenarios of business use cases can be described with activity diagrams. If a business use case is composed of several different scenarios, each is depicted in an activity diagram.

The following checklist shows the steps necessary for constructing activity diagrams:

Checklist 3.3 Constructing Activity Diagrams in the External View:

- Collect information sources—How am I supposed to know that?
- Find activities and actions—What has to be done when actors draw upon offered goods and services?
- Adopt actors from business use cases—Who is responsible for each action?
- Connect actions—In which order are actions processed?
- Refine activities—Do any other activity diagrams have to be added?
- Verify the view—Is everything correct?

The order in which we present these steps was chosen deliberately. However, the order is not mandatory, since in practice the individual work steps often overlap heavily.

Collect Information Sources—How am I Supposed to Know That?

For the construction of activity diagrams we can use information that has already been collected for the construction of use case diagrams. Otherwise, the same advice holds true as in Section 3. *Constructing Use Case Diagrams*.

Find Activities and Actions—What has to be Done When Actors Draw upon Offered Goods and Services?

Here too, we can start from a use case diagram. In the first step, we can derive activities from business use cases. Answering the following questions will help you find activities and actions:

- Which work steps are required to carry out a business use case, meaning which steps are required to supply and process goods and services?

- What do the individual actors do?

- If several actors are involved in a business use case, which work steps are performed by each individual actor?

- Which events initiate which work steps?

- Which actions are so extensive that they have to be refined in another activity diagram?

In our case study, you can find the following work steps for passenger services:

- Passenger checks in (derived from use case diagram); this entails issuing a boarding pass though passenger services.

- Passenger boards airplane (derived from use case diagram).

In addition to this, there are other steps and events:

- Passenger arrives at check-in counter and shows his or her ticket; this event initiates the check-in activity.

- Luggage is loaded into the airplane by baggage transportation.

At first, just as above, activities can be described in an informal manner. We often find pre-existing documentation of processes, either informal or structured, which can be used as a basis to find activities and actions.

Connect Actions—In Which Order are Actions Processed?

Connecting the previously mentioned actions and activities into a flow generates an initial activity diagram. This flow is called **control flow**. The following questions will help you develop a control flow:

- In which order are actions processed?

- Which conditions have to be met in order for an action to be executed?

- Where are branches necessary?

- Which actions occur simultaneously?

- Is the completion of actions necessary before the flow can proceed to other actions?

Passenger checks in, **passenger boards**, and **loading luggage into airplane** are complex activities, each of which is detailed in another activity diagram. The 'fork' within the action symbols indicates this:

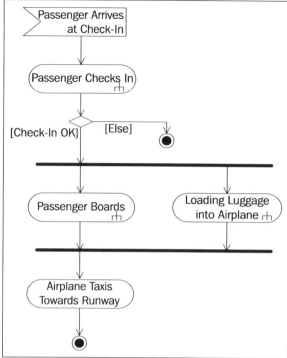

Figure 3.19 A high-level activity diagram across several business use cases

Refine Activities—Do any Other Activity Diagrams have to be Added?

As we could see in Figure 3.19, it is necessary to refine several process steps. Here, we would like to display the activity of **passenger checks in** in more detail.

When a passenger checks in, he or she first shows his or her ticket at the check-in counter. The ticket will be checked for its validity. If the ticket is not OK the passenger will be referred to customer service. If the ticket is OK the passenger will check his or her luggage. If the luggage has excess weight he or she will pay an additional fee. The luggage will be forwarded to baggage transportation. The passenger receives his or her boarding pass.

Determine the level of detail in activity diagrams very consciously. Test which level of detail users of the diagrams can stand and which is the least amount of detail necessary. We cannot give universally valid rules, since the level of detail essentially depends on the target group and purpose of the model.

Now, we have the following additional actions (Figure 3.20):

Figure 3.20 Actions of an activity with a higher level of detail

Adopt Actors from Business Use Cases—Who is Responsible for Each Action?

In business processes it is important to know who is responsible for each individual action and who carries it out (Figure 3.21):

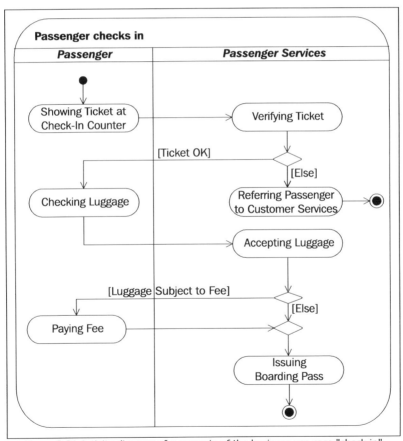

Figure 3.21 Activity diagram of a scenario of the business use case "check-in"

For the external view actors are adopted from the use case diagram. Each actor is responsible for a certain action and is recorded in a partition (swimlane) as the responsible party.

The individual activities are assigned to the responsible parties. The division of the activity diagram into partitions allows a clear overview of responsibilities. However, partitions can also be formed on the basis of other criteria.

An activity diagram could, for instance, be divided in such a way that manual, automated, and semi-automated actions would each make up one partition. This would be a good foundation for the conversion of flows into IT systems.

Verify the View—Is Everything Correct?

Just like use case diagrams, activity diagrams also have to be verified in terms of correctness of content, in cooperation with knowledge carriers.

> **Checklist Verifying Activity Diagrams in the External View**:
>
> - When constructing activity diagrams from the external view, always remember that internal procedures and business processes are irrelevant. Restrict your consideration to the description of those functionalities of the business system that are utilized by outsiders.
> - The conditions of different outputs should not overlap. Otherwise, the control flow is ambiguous, meaning that it is not clear where the flow proceeds after a decision node.
> - The conditions have to include all possibilities; otherwise, the control flow can get stuck. In case of doubt, insert an output with the condition 'else'.
> - Forks and joins should be well balanced. The number of flows that leave a branch should match the number of flows that end in the corresponding join.

3.3.7 Sequence Diagrams

UML provides two types of diagrams for the representation of interactions: the sequence diagram and the communication diagram. Both diagrams visualize the exchange of information. However, the emphasis is different: **communication diagrams** emphasize the relationships of individual objects and their topology; **sequence diagrams** emphasize the chronological course of exchanged information. In the external view, we opt for the representation through sequence diagrams and do without communication diagrams for two reasons:

- Sequence diagrams are easier to understand for developers and readers. In our practical work in projects we have observed a much higher acceptance of sequence diagrams because of their simplicity.

- We avoid using unnecessarily many diagram types for the same facts. Less is often more!

If a customer or business partner uses an offered service, partners communicate with each other. The process can be described as a series of interactions. These interactions are clearly laid out in the sequence diagram, whereas the activities of each partner and the conditions under which the interactions take place are omitted in the diagram. However, they can be described with supplementary comments.

Like the activity diagrams, sequence diagrams can be modeled spanning several use cases, as well as being used to refine business use cases. A sequence diagram illustrates the various scenarios of a business use case.

Sequence diagrams can be used as the basis for message exchange between the business system and outside parties (Figure 3.22). We will treat this topic in Chapter 5, *Modeling for System Integration*:

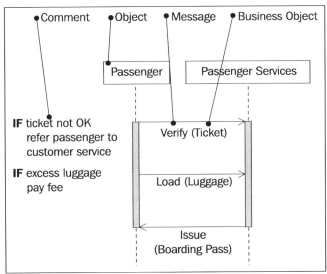

Figure 3.22 The elements of the sequence diagram

In a sequence diagram, we work with the following elements:

Comment: Sequence diagrams can be annotated with comments (UML generally permits comments in all diagrams.):

> **IF** ticket not OK
>   refer passenger to
>   customer service
> ...

For instance, activities of partners or conditions can be specified as comments.

Object: Objects that are involved in interactions are placed on the *x*-axis. Objects are senders and receivers of messages in the sequence diagram:

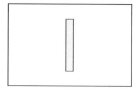

In the business system model (external view) these objects represent the actors of the business system and the business system itself.

Message and Business Object: The messages that objects send and receive are shown on the *y*-axis. Messages are inserted in increasing chronological order from top to bottom. The direction of the arrow indicates the direction in which a message is sent:

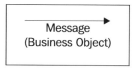

The business object is listed in parenthesis. Business objects are conveyed together with messages. Some examples of business objects are tickets, boarding passes, and luggage. These examples will be treated in more detail in Section .2, *Package Diagram*.

Reading Sequence Diagrams

Figure 3.23 shows a sequence diagram with the objects **passenger** and **passenger services**. The entire diagram documents the process of the business use case **passenger check-in**.

You begin reading a sequence diagram at the top (1). The starting point on the top left (1) is located on the vertical line that represents the **passenger** (2) as sender and receiver of messages. The flow begins when the **passenger** hands over his or her **ticket** (3) to **passenger services** for **verification** (4). The call **verify** (4) is the message; the **ticket** (3) that is handed over is the business object. The direction of the arrow indicates that the **passenger** is the sender of the message and **passenger services** the **receiver** (6).

The receipt of the message at passenger services initiates activities, which is indicated by the gray vertical bar (7). The diagram does not show how passenger services handle the process, meaning that it does not show which activities are conducted:

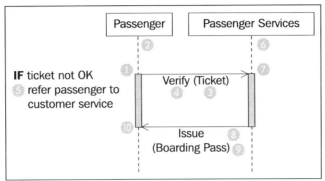

Figure 3.23 Sequence diagram "Passenger Check-In"

Only the comment (5) can include a clue. Comments can be inserted at the left margin of the sequence diagram. An exact description of the processing can be found in the activity diagram 'passenger checks in' (see Figure 3.21 above).

In a final step, passenger services **issues** (8) a **boarding pass** (9) to the passenger. With that, the interaction that is illustrated in this sequence diagram is completed for both parties. This is indicated by the end of the wide gray vertical bar (10).

In the business model we do not utilize all the options of the sequence diagram. UML provides many more possibilities for this diagram type, but our experience showed that this is sufficient to communicate the essential aspects.

3.3.8 Constructing Sequence Diagrams

The following checklist shows the necessary steps for the construction of sequence diagrams. Subsequently, we will further explain the individual steps.

Checklist 3.5 Constructing Sequence Diagrams in the External View:

- Designate actors and business system—Who is taking part?
- Designate initiators—Who starts interactions?
- Describe the message exchange between actors and business system—Which messages are being exchanged?
- Identify the course of interactions—What is the order?
- Insert additional information—What else is important?
- Verify the view—Is everything correct?

Designate Actors and Business System—Who is Taking Part?

Sequence diagrams illustrate the interactions between actors and the business system. Fundamentally we have a pool of interaction partners from the use case diagrams. Depending on the flow that is being depicted in the sequence diagram, the appropriate actors and business systems can be selected from this pool.

In our case study (see Figure 3.24), we find the interaction partners **passenger** and **passenger services** for the above sequence diagram (Figure 3.23):

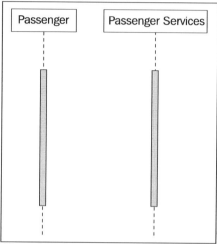

Figure 3.24 Constructing sequence diagrams

Designate Initiators—Who Starts Interactions?

For every sequence of interactions the actor who starts the interaction has to be identified. This actor is called the **initiator**. Since in the external view of the business model each business use case is initiated by an actor, we can here also select the actor from the pool of actors in the use case diagrams.

In our sequence diagram passenger check-in, the passenger starts the interaction by utilizing the service check-in from passenger services.

Describe the Message Exchange between Actors and the Business System—Which Messages are being Exchanged?

After the initiator has been defined, the subsequent progression of interactions has to be identified. For each communication step it has to be determined what information is exchanged. In this way the message will be defined. Messages are requests to do something directed toward a particular partner. The business objects that are exchanged with these messages also have to be defined.

Identify the Course of Interactions—What is the Order?

All messages are exchanged in a chronological order that has to be identified. Messages are inserted along the *y*-axis in increasing chronological order, from top to bottom (see Figure 3.25):

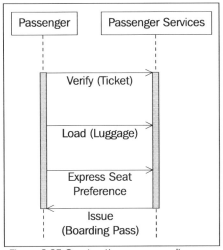

Figure 3.25 Constructing sequence diagrams

Insert Additional Information—What Else is Important?

Important activities of involved actors and business systems and important conditions can be inserted into the diagram as comments. Comments are inserted at the level of the appropriate message. Restrict this to important comments that have significance so that the diagram is not overcrowded with text (see Figure 3.26):

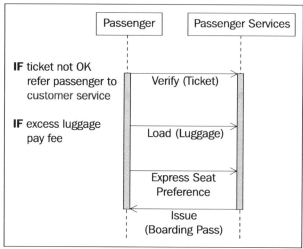

Figure 3.26 Constructing sequence diagrams

Verify the View—Is Everything Correct?

Completed sequence diagrams can be verified with the following checklist:

Checklist 3.6 Verifying Sequence Diagrams in the External View:

- Are all required sequence diagrams completed and available? There should be a sequence diagram for each business use case.
- Are the sequence diagrams correct? Each sequence diagram contains only one object that represents the business system, and at most as many other objects as there are actors assigned to the business use case.
- Is each actor that is listed in the use case diagram mentioned in at least one sequence diagram?
- Is each actor who initiates a business use case mentioned as a starting point in one of the sequence diagrams?
- Have all the important comments been inserted into the diagram? Are there maybe too many comments inserted into the diagram thereby reducing its clarity?

3.3.9 High-Level Sequence Diagrams

We can use high-level sequence diagrams that span several business use cases to illustrate business processes at a coarse level. High-level sequence diagrams give a good overview of the interactions between customers, partners, and the business system. They serve as the basis for the electronic data transfer between the business system and customers, business partners, and suppliers (see Chapter 5, *Modeling for System Integration*).

Figure 3.27 illustrates passenger services. The entire process spans the business use cases **check-in** and **boarding**:

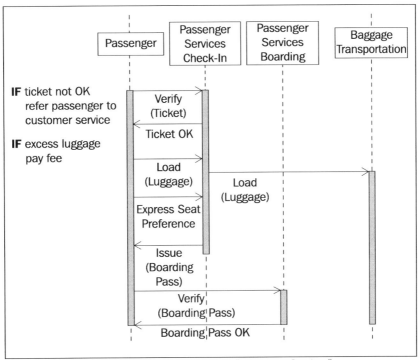

Figure 3.27 Sequence diagram "Passenger Services"

3.3.10 Sequence Diagrams for Scenarios of Business Use Cases

Sequence diagrams assist the detailing and specification of business use cases by emphasizing message exchange. The various scenarios of a business use case can be depicted in a sequence diagram. The representation is restricted to the message exchange within each business use case. Generally, the level of detail for these sequence diagrams is higher than for sequence diagrams spanning use cases.

Figure 3.28 shows a sequence diagram of the business use case **check-in**. This sequence diagram shows the scenario **passenger check-in**, as can be seen from the communication partners since the check-in representative does not appear. Sequence diagrams, just like activity diagrams, show if actors can carry out business use cases together or independently of one another (which cannot be seen in use case diagrams):

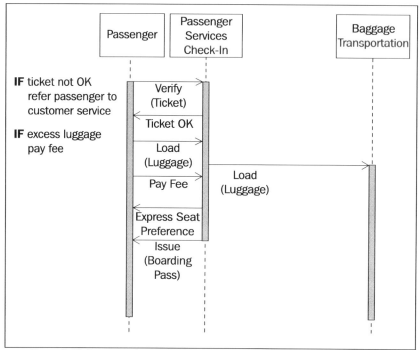

Figure 3.28 Sequence diagram of the business use case "Passenger Check-In"

The Internal View

The internal view describes the internal **processes** and **activities**, **relationships**, and **structures** of the business system. IT systems and people within the business system are responsible for offering the goods and services of the business system. With that, we leave the environment of the business system and enter the black box. From now on, we do care about whether the processing within the business system occurs manually or is IT supported, whether employees of the organization have to fill out two or twenty forms, and whether suppliers are needed.

3.4.1 The Elements of the View

The following diagrams illustrate the internal view:

- **Package diagrams** describe the organization units in the form of packages.

- **Class diagrams** describe the connections and relationships between co-workers and business objects.

- **Activity diagrams** describe the business processes within the business system. The subjects of the description are the goods and services that are provided by internal business system resources (see Figure 3.29):

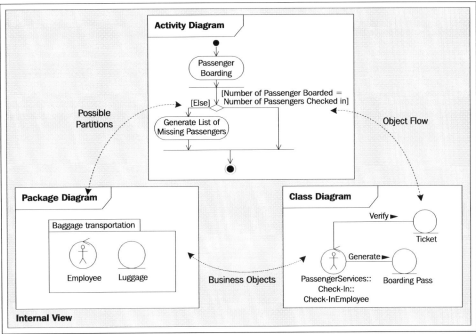

Figure 3.29 Diagram types of the internal view of the business system

3.4.2 Package Diagram

The structure of organization units is important for the internal view of the business system. In UML, organization units are depicted as packages, which can contain employees, business objects, and other organization units. In our case study, we chose the organization unit passenger services (see Figure 3.30):

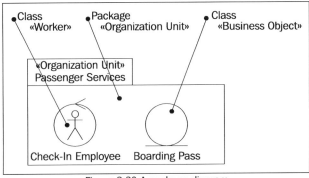

Figure 3.30 A package diagram

Organization units can be responsible for the execution of business-process activities. Organization units are abstractions of individual jobs within an organization.

In UML an organization unit spans workers, business objects, other organization units, and their relationships. As a basic principle, organization units are located within business systems. Organization units that are located outside business systems are actors.

In package diagrams we work with the following elements:

Package «Organization Unit»

Organization units are depicted as packages. In the small box in the upper left the name of the organization unit is inserted below the stereotype **«Organization Unit»**:

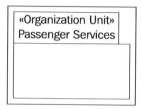

The content of organization units is inserted into the main box. Most of the time, it is sufficient to list the most important elements (employees, business objects).

Class «Worker»

The stereotype **«Worker»** is used to describe the roles of those people who execute business processes or who are involved in the execution of business processes:

We are not concerned with the 'status' of workers, such as salaried employee, free-lancer, or volunteer, but with their roles, meaning jobs. Workers are responsible for providing goods and services. They are located within a business system. Here, the following characteristics are important:

- Workers are people.
- Workers are located within the business system.
- Workers can communicate with other workers and with actors outside the business system.

Workers can have their own symbol; below the worker symbol the role of the worker is inserted. The symbol shows an actor symbol that is surrounded by a circle—this is supposed to indicate that the worker is located *within* something. The worker symbol can also be omitted. In this case, the class symbol is used and the term **«worker»** is written as a stereotype in angle brackets.

«Business Object»

Business objects are **passive**, meaning they do not initiate interactions. Business objects can be involved in several different business use cases and outlive individual interactions. This makes them a form of connecting link between business use cases or workers that are involved in various use cases:

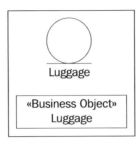

Workers handle (utilize, control, manipulate, produce, etc) handle business objects. In our case study business objects are, for instance, a ticket, a piece of luggage, or a boarding pass. Business objects are also illustrated with their own symbol; the description of the business object is written below the business object symbol.

The business object symbol can also be omitted. In this case, the class symbol is used and the term **«Business Object»** is written as a stereotype in angle brackets.

Reading Package Diagrams

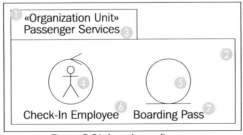

Figure 3.31 A package diagram

Through the stereotype **«Organization Unit»** (1) you can see that the package (2) represents an organization unit. The name of this organization unit is **passenger services** (3). Within this organization unit you can find the **check-in employee** (4) and the business object: **boarding pass** (5). The graphic symbol (4) on the left represents a **worker**; the label (6) below the graphic symbol indicates the **worker's role** within the organization. The graphic symbol (5) on the right represents a **business object**; the label (7) below the graphic symbol indicates the **type** of business object we are dealing with.

There is only *one* symbol for the check-in employee. That doesn't mean there is only one check-in employee, but rather the symbol represents a role that can be fulfilled by any number of real check-in employees. Surely, there are other worker roles within passenger services (manager, assistant, etc.). However, these are irrelevant for the illustration of our processes, and so do not have to be included in the package diagram (see Figure 3.31).

3.4.3 Constructing Package Diagrams

The following checklist shows the steps that are necessary for the construction of package diagrams. Subsequently, we will further explain the individual steps.

Checklist 3.7 Constructing Package Diagrams in the Internal View:

- Develop an initial package diagram of the business system—Which workers and business objects make up the business system?
- Find additional organization units—Who else is there?
- Assign workers and business objects to the organization units—Who belongs where?
- Find additional organization units, workers, or business objects—What else is there?
- Verify the view—Is everything correct?

Develop an Initial Package Diagram of the Business System—Which Workers and Business Objects Make up the Business System?

At first, the entire business system makes up the organization unit that is supposed to be depicted. In our case, this is passenger services (see Figure 3.32). Initially, we search for relevant worker roles (jobs) and business objects for this organization unit. Existing job descriptions and organization charts can be helpful for this:

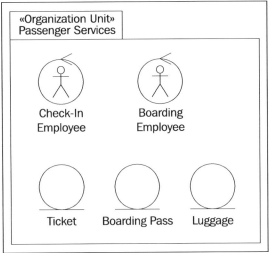

Figure 3.32 Constructing a package diagram

Find Additional Organization Units—Who Else is There?

Potentially, the organization unit can be divided into further organization units (divisions, teams, groups). You can use organization charts and job descriptions as the basis and select the organization units that are relevant for the model. Relevant organization units and jobs are those that are directly integrated into the processing of goods and services.

In our case study, we divide passenger service in further organization units: check-in and boarding. A further division is only wise if it is important for the illustration of business processes. For instance, a secretary pool is not important for the business processes under consideration.

Assign Workers and Business Objects to the Organization Units—Who Belongs Where?

Employees and business objects have to be assigned to the additional organization units. You can see in Figure 3.33 that the business objects were divided. Because of this, structure and assignments are clearly recognizable.

Find Additional Organization Units, Workers, or Business Objects—What Else is There?

UML package diagrams representing organization units should not be confused with organization charts. In fact, organization charts are related to package diagrams as they are shown here. However, package diagrams contain business objects in addition to employees. From organization charts we can derive hierarchical structure and the roles of the various workers, and use them as the basis for the construction of package diagrams:

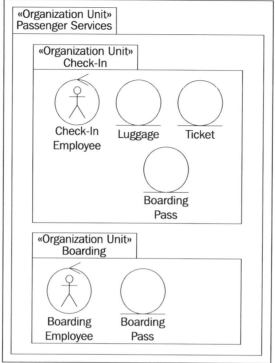

Figure 3.33 Organization unit "Passenger Services"

Verify the View—Is Everything Correct?

The completed package diagram can be checked with the following checklist:

Checklist 3.8 Verifying Package Diagrams in the Internal View:

- Are all workers and organization units that are affected by the processing of goods and services provided by the business system included in the package diagram?
- Are there no workers and organization units that are unrelated to the processing of goods and services of the business system included in the package diagram?
- Are all business objects that are needed for providing and processing goods and services included in the package diagram?
- Are there no business objects that are unrelated to the processing of goods and services of the business system included in the package diagram?

3.4.4 Class Diagram

The class diagram can be used to illustrate the structural parts of a business system, meaning the relationships between individual employees, business objects, and outside parties. We significantly simplify class diagrams on the business-model level and use only very few elements. It still holds true: less is often more! When the manifold options of class diagrams are used, these diagrams are no longer easy to read. On the business-system level we have to act on the assumption that involved parties have little or no IT expertise and know nothing about class terminology and class diagrams. The expected advantage of UML, namely easier communication between the various involved parties, would be significantly impaired. For a deeper explanation of class diagrams, refer to Chapter 4, *Modeling IT Systems*:

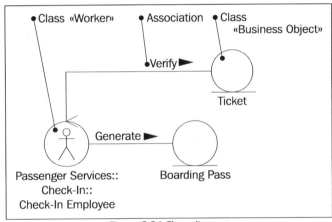

Figure 3.34 Class diagram

In class diagrams we work with only a few elements:

Class «Worker»

We have already described the class **worker** in Section 3.4.2, *Package Diagram*. Those are exactly the same classes as the ones we use here in the class diagram; just as in the package diagram, they can be depicted with the worker symbol or the class symbol:

As you can see in Figure 3.34, you can state the entire path name of a class to illustrate membership of a package. In our example, the entire path signifies that the class **check -in employee** belongs to the package **check-in**, and that the package **check-in** belongs to the package **passenger services**, each divided by a double colon. The class **worker** is used in the class diagram to illustrate relationships with other employees, actors, and business objects.

Class «Business Object»

We have already described the class **business object** in Section 3.4.2, *Package Diagram*. Those are exactly the same classes as the ones we use here in the class diagram:

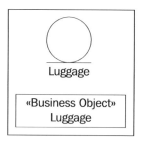

Just as in the package diagram, they can be depicted with the business object symbol or the class symbol.

Association

An association represents a relationship that has a precisely defined meaning. The association can be labeled with the name of the association. If you want to assign a direction to the association's name, you can insert a triangle that points to the direction in which the name is supposed to be read:

In addition to the above-mentioned elements, we would like to mention the generalization. However, we do not think that the use of this element is mandatory.

Generalization

A generalization is a specific relationship between a general and a specific element. Generalization and specialization help with hierarchical structuring. If several business objects are supposed to be combined to one comprehensive item, generalization is the right tool (see Figure 3.35):

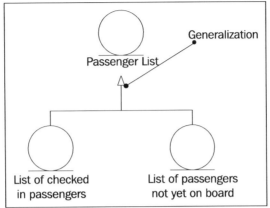

However, for workers we recommend structuring in package diagrams:

Figure 3.35 Class diagram with generalization

Reading Class Diagrams

Figure 3.36 shows a small excerpt of a class diagram from our case study.
It contains the classes **check-in employee** (1), **ticket** (2), and **boarding pass** (3), as well as their associations:

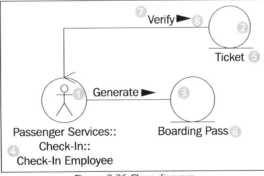

Figure 3.36 Class diagram

You can see by the label (4) of the worker symbol (1), that the check-in employee belongs to the organization unit check-in, which is a division of passenger services.

The labels that are written in front of the label for the worker, separated by double colons, indicate the organization units that the workers belong to. You can see that passenger services and check-in are organization units from the package diagram.

The labels of the business object symbols (5 and 6) show that we have two business objects: **ticket** (5) and **boarding pass** (6).

Associations between classes should be read in the following manner:

- A check-in employee (4) verifies (7) a ticket (5).

The small triangle (8) next to the name of the association (7) indicates the **direction** in which the name of the association is supposed to be read. All associations within class diagrams can be read in this way.

We do not use any multiplicities in class diagrams of the business-system model, meaning, for the benefit of clarity, we do not make any statements about the number of objects in classes that are involved in associations.

It is not yet important if a check-in employee issues one or several boarding passes. Important quantities can be included as comments. Quantities will be of interest later: in the IT-system model, which will be described in Chapter 4, *Modeling IT Systems*.

3.4.5 Constructing Class Diagrams

The following steps have to be executed for the construction of class diagrams:

Checklist 3.9 Constructing Class Diagrams in the Internal View:

- Find classes—Which classes exist in the class diagram?
- Create associations between classes—Which classes deal with each other?
- Substantiate associations—What do these relationships mean?
- Insert generalizations—Can business objects be grouped?
- Verify the view—Is everything correct?

Find Classes—Which Classes Exist in the Class Diagram?

You can use the classes of package diagrams for the class diagram of the business system's internal view, meaning workers and business objects. Actors from use case diagrams are also classes that can be adopted into this class diagram. In our example, you'll find the classes that are displayed in Figure 3.37:

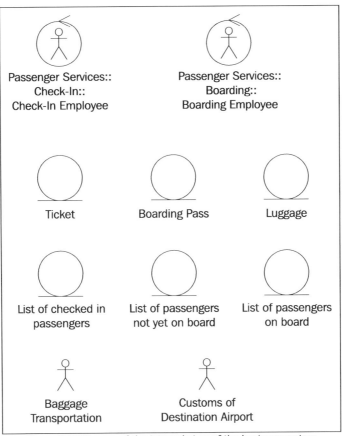

Figure 3.37 Classes of the internal view of the business system

Create Associations Between Classes—Which Classes Deal with Each Other?

In class diagrams, the relationships between the found classes as well as business rules are modeled as associations.

The question is:

- What relationships exist between workers, business objects, and other objects?

Even though we begin with the classes that have already been found, we usually find more classes in this work step through domain discussions.

Substantiate Associations—What do these Relationships Mean?

Associations between individual classes have to be labeled with meaningful names, so that the class diagram can be understood easily and intuitively. Generally, a direction is added to the association, according to which it can be read (see Figure 3.38).

Insert Generalizations—Can Business Objects be Grouped?

It might make sense to group business objects into another higher-ranking class. In our case study, it is helpful to illustrate that the list of checked-in passengers, the list of passengers on board, and the list of passengers not yet on board, are of the type «**Passenger List**» (see Figure 3.39):

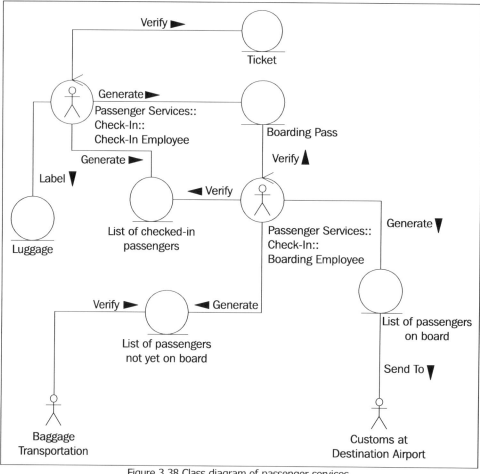

Figure 3.38 Class diagram of passenger services

This shows that the lists have the same structure (also see Section 4.2.2, *Generalization, Specialization, and Heredity* in Chapter 4):

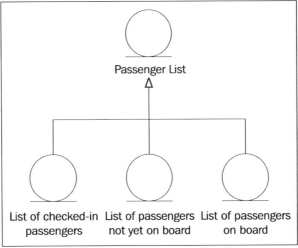

Figure 3.39 Generalization in the class diagram

Verify the View—Is Everything Correct?

The completed class diagram can be verified with the following checklist:

Checklist 3.10 Verifying Class Diagrams in the Internal View:

- Is the class diagram complete? Are all classes from the package diagram also present in the class diagram?
- Are all associations labeled in a meaningful way? Are the directions of the arrows correct?
- Is the class diagram correct? Intensive reading in collaboration with knowledge carriers and a run-through of each service will bring to light most mistakes.
- Is the level of detail optimized? Is the diagram detailed enough to cover everything, or is the diagram too detailed and obscure because it lacks clarity in certain aspects?

3.4.6 Activity Diagram

Activity diagrams are suitable to show the internal processes of a business system. Contrary to activity diagrams of the external view, in activity diagrams of the internal view the relationships to actors are no longer the focal point.

Activity diagrams of the internal view are also suitable as a basis for instructions.

Reading Activity Diagrams

The reading instructions in Section 3.3.5, *Activity Diagrams*, can be used for activity diagrams of the internal view.

3.4.7 Constructing Activity Diagrams

Essentially, the construction of activity diagrams of the internal view takes place exactly like the construction of activity diagrams of the external view.

The following checklist and the explanations of the individual steps are adapted to the modified view.

Checklist 3.11 Constructing Activity Diagrams in the Internal View:

- Collect information sources—How am I supposed to know that?
- Find activities and actions—Which activities have to be performed so that the goods and services utilized by actors can be provided and delivered?
- Adopt actors from business use cases—Who is responsible for each action?
- Connect actions—In which order are actions processed?
- Refine activities—Do any other activity diagrams have to be added?
- Verify the view—Is everything correct?

Collect Information Sources—How am I Supposed to Know That?

When constructing activity diagrams of the internal view, the same directions as in Section 3.3.4, *Constructing Use Case Diagrams*, hold true in order to obtain the necessary information.

Find Activities and Actions—Which Activities Have to be Performed so that the Goods and Services Utilized by Actors can be Provided and Delivered?

Here, we can borrow from use cases and actions of activity diagrams of the external view. We have to ask the following question for the individual business processes that are depicted in the external view: How does the internal processing take place and what do the internal business processes look like? Answering the following questions will help you find activities and actions:

- Which work steps have to be performed by employees of the business system to provide and deliver a service?
- What does each employee do?
- Which outside events initiate which activities and actions?

Often, we can find pre-existing documentation of flows, either informal or structured, that we can use to find activities.

Adopt Actors from Business Use Cases—Who is Responsible for Each Action?

Predominantly, workers and organization units from the package diagram are responsible for the actions. Actors from use case diagrams are also used, as long as they are involved in the depicted business processes.

Each worker, each organization unit, and each actor is responsible for certain activities and is inserted into an activity partition (swimlane) as the responsible party. The individual actions are assigned to these responsibilities.

If activity diagrams are refined, it is possible that other areas of responsibility will be added, for example, individual positions or teams.

Connect Actions—In Which Order are Actions Processed?

Connecting the individual actions in a flow generates an initial activity diagram, which describes internal business processes. The following questions help with the construction of the control flow:

- In which order are actions processed?
- Which conditions have to be met in order for an action to be executed?

- Where are branches necessary?
- Which actions occur simultaneously?
- Is the completion of some actions necessary before the flow can proceed to other actions?

Refine Activities—Do any Other Activity Diagrams Have to be Added?

It is possible that individual actions have to be further divided or refined with other activity diagrams. Different scenarios are also described in other activity diagrams.

Verify the View—Is Everything Correct?

Activity diagrams of the internal view also have to be verified in terms of correctness of content. This should be done in collaboration with knowledge carriers.

Checklist 3.12 Verifying Activity Diagrams of the Internal View:

- When constructing activity diagrams of the external view, always remember that only internal procedures and business processes are relevant.
- The conditions of different outputs of a decision node should not overlap. Otherwise, the control flow is ambiguous—it is not clear where the flow proceeds after a decision node.
- The conditions have to include all possibilities. Otherwise, the control flow can get stuck. In case of doubt, insert an output with the condition 'else'.
- Forks and joins should be well balanced. The number of flows that leave a fork should match the number of flows that end in the corresponding join.

In the following Figure 3.40 depicts an activity diagram that represents the internal processing of the activities accepting luggage during check-in by passenger services:

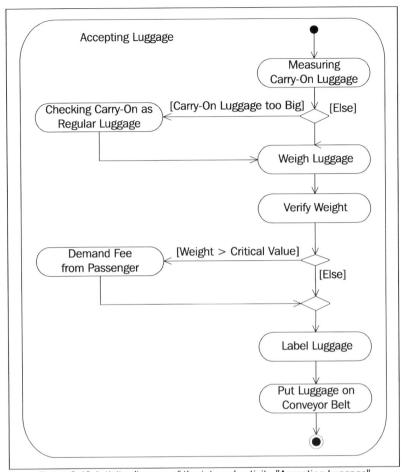

Figure 3.40 Activity diagram of the internal activity "Accepting Luggage"

The activity **accepting luggage**, as shown in Figure 3.40, is carried out by passenger services. It is not important for the passenger or for baggage transportation which actions are performed in what way. The passenger is only interested in whether his or her carry-on is too big and if he or she has to pay for excess weight; baggage transportation needs labels on each piece of luggage. All other details that are shown in the diagram are internal processing details of passenger services and will therefore be labelled as 'internal view'.

4

Modeling IT Systems

Modeling is the foundation for successful development and implementation of new IT systems. A correct and complete model ensures that, in the end, users get the IT system they need.

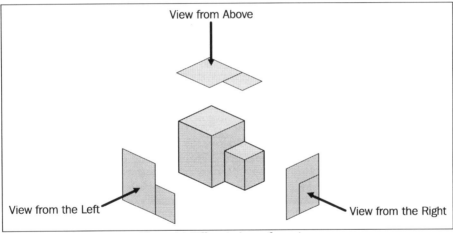

Figure 4.1 Different views of a system

In this chapter, we show how a **conceptual model** of an IT system can be developed with the help of UML. Taking into consideration the 80:20 rule, we do not use all the features of UML. Practice shows that it is unrealistic to model everything in full depth with UML. This is because in the implementation stage new insights are gained, which cannot be foreseen during the conception stage. In addition to that, models should be developed with the least amount of effort possible.

The IT system model consists of four different views, each of which emphasizes certain aspects and which are closely related to each other. This approach of a model consisting of different views, is illustrated in Figure 4.1.The individual views we use for the IT system model, and the UML diagrams included in them are depicted in Figure 4.2:

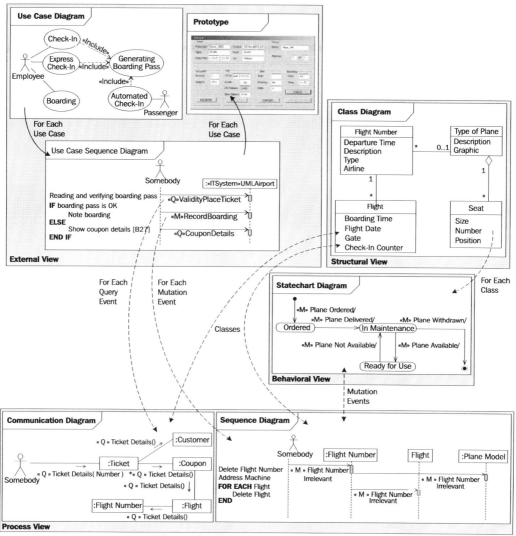

Figure 4.2 Different views of an IT system

- External View—Use case diagram and use case sequence diagram
- Structural View—Class diagram
- Interaction View—Sequence diagram and communication diagram
- Behavioral View—Statechart diagram

Each of these views emphasizes certain aspects, and thus, disregards all others. All the views combined make up a fairly complete model of the functionality of an IT system:

- The **external view** shows the use cases of the IT system in the form of UML use case diagrams and an interface prototype. It makes apparent which functionalities the IT system provides to users.

- The **structural view** shows the relevant classes of the IT system in the form of UML class diagrams. It makes apparent in which structures information is filed in the IT system.

- The **behavioral view** shows the behavior of the individual objects in the form of statechart diagrams. It makes apparent everything that can happen with an object that is filed in the IT system.

- The **interaction view** shows flows that take place during mutations or queries within the IT system, in the form of sequence diagrams and communication diagrams. It makes apparent what takes place in the IT system when a user utilizes it.

Events are the real links that hold the different views together. They are contained in three of the four views:

- In the **external view** the individual use cases are described as a sequence of events that are sent to the IT system.

- The **behavioral view** shows for each class how the objects respond to the events that reach them.

- The **interaction view** shows how the individual events in the IT system are relayed to the affected objects.

Only in the class diagram of the structural view are events not visible. The class diagram shows classes and the relationships, but not the dynamic aspects between them.

We do not use all types of diagrams that UML provides to model IT systems. In practice, the combination of diagrams that we describe in this chapter has proven to be valuable for modeling IT systems. A consistent and complete model of the IT system can be developed with these diagrams. For other models the optimal combination of diagrams looks different. For instance, activity diagrams have proven to be valuable for the business system model.

In the following sections, we will discuss the four views individually. In practice, the development of these four views does not simply follow this order. Rather, working on each view will provide new insights for the other views. The dashed arrows in Figure 4.2 show the most important of these relationships.

4.1 External View

4.1.1 The User View or "I don't care how it works, as long as it works."

If today someone uses a modern piece of equipment, for example a video recorder, an ATM, or a cell phone, he or she is rarely interested in how that piece of equipment looks from the inside. The average user does not care which electronic parts a machine consists of, or what software it includes. On the other hand, what the machine can be used for, or what functionalities it provides, is important to the user. For instance, the buyer of a cell phone wants to know if the device has WAP capability or how many addresses it can store. Usually, the potential buyer of a cell phone is interested in how the device can be used; he or she is not interested in how the device is built internally, as long as it has the desired functionalities.

This type of view of a system is called a **black-box view**, meaning the system or device is pictured as a black box—you cannot look inside. You don't know how it works; you only know that it does work. Ideally, this is the view a user should have of an IT system. He or she uses the IT system to complete his or her work, just like a coffee maker or copier. He or she knows what can be done with the system, and usually also knows how to do it.

The external view is an essential part of the IT system model. Here, it is determined what future users expect from the IT system. The functionality that is defined in this view should ultimately be used to verify if the IT system fulfils the requirements.

The external view consists of the elements use case diagrams, use case sequence diagrams, and interface prototypes. At first sight, these elements appear strange. Some analysts may be tempted to allege that it is sufficient to record user requirements in the form of prose. But practical experience shows again and again that this is not true. Prose can be inconsistent, imprecise, and incomplete, without it becoming obvious to the future user when he or she reads it. The IT system is developed accordingly and the programmer interprets the prose as a third party, from his or her own viewpoint, and implements the system accordingly. The UML-defined diagrams that we describe and explain in this chapter are meant to help avoid misunderstandings and misinterpretations. The diagrams are tools to describe the requirements for an IT system.

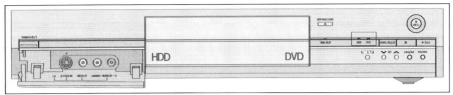

Figure 4.3 External view of a system as black box

An essential element of a system is its user interface. The user interface of an ATM, for example, consists of a small monitor, the keys, and the openings for cards, bills, and receipts, as well as the beep.

The user interface is the only access point that a user has to a system. If, for instance, the recording button of a video recorder is missing, it is impossible to record anything, even if the video recorder is equipped for this function internally.

The user interface represents a type of view of the functionality of the device. What is missing in this view is inaccessible.

However, the user interface gives a static view of the system. This view does not show how the system is supposed to be used, and which operating elements have to be used in which order to complete a certain task.

Because of this, user interfaces require instruction manuals. This means that we need a description that identifies the actions that are possible and what sequence has to be followed for the system to be used in a meaningful manner. In UML, these courses of actions are called use cases. **Use cases** are instruction manuals for the user interface. Only what is defined in an instruction manual is a meaningful course of action.

The following example is a meaningful course of action (flow) for the use of a phone: picking up receiver, waiting for the dial tone, typing a valid phone number, waiting for someone to answer the phone, talking, and hanging up.

Flows that are not defined in the instruction manual are not regarded as meaningful and are not supported by the system. In poorly developed systems, it can happen that flows that are not defined have unexpected consequences or even crash the system.

Sometimes, modern IT systems can solve ad hoc problems, especially queries. Because of their nature, ad hoc use cases are not included in normal descriptions. Other solutions have to be found for them, for example, the specification of an environment or of a specific system that supports ad hoc queries. Instead of a description, ad hoc use cases receive a reference to a reporting tool or query language.

For users, a system essentially consists of a user interface and use cases, even though these generally only represent the tip of the iceberg. Everything beyond that is of no interest for users. Or did you ever ponder what type of system is behind the keys of your cell phone?

> Write down the use cases of a system that you deal with on a general basis. Such a system could be, for instance, an ATM, a coffee maker, or a web portal.

Figure 4.4 Actor who is carrying out a use case

The best approach to model the use cases of an IT system is precisely to imagine a user who sits in front of the keyboard and works with the IT system (see Figure 4.4). The user becomes the actor, and the use case is nothing more than an abstract description of the user's activity.

An actor:

- Interacts directly with a system
- Is always located outside the system with which he or she interacts

For the IT system, this means that the actor is always the one who directly operates the IT system.

Even in higher-ranking business systems (see Chapter 3, *Modeling Business Systems*) actors are located on the outside. They can be, for example, customers or partners.

The worker who operates the IT system, on the other hand, is part of the business system. Because of this, he or she cannot be an actor of the business system:

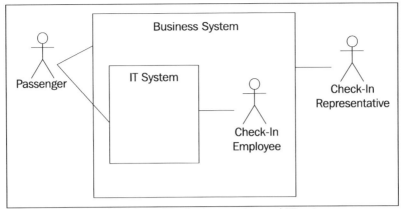

Figure 4.5 Actors of the business system and IT system

This leads to the situation shown in Figure 4.5:

- A **passenger** is actor of the business system, and generally deals with a check-in employee. However, he or she can also be a firsthand actor of the IT system, for example, during automated check-in at a machine.

- A **check-in employee** is part of the business system. Because of this he or she is not an actor of the business system. On the other hand, as user he or she is an actor of the IT system.

- A **check-in representative**, who performs check-in in place of another person, is only an actor of the business system, because he or she cannot perform automated check-in and therefore never has direct contact with the IT system.

In summary, we can say that actors and use cases are very well suited to communicate with users or domain experts about the functionality of IT systems that is visible from the outside.

In our Hanseatic merchant's trading office, the separation between business system and IT system is somewhat difficult. However, you can consider that the clerk's office with the clerks and secretary Hildebrand make up the functionality of an information system (without IT). A use case then, would correspond with a work process of secretary Hildebrand, such as updating payment receipts or summarizing the costs and revenues of last month. Here, the actor is the owner, Mr. Hafenstein (see Figure 4.6):

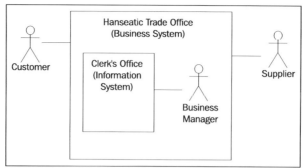

Figure 4.6 Actors in the Hanseatic trade office

4.1.2 The Elements of a View

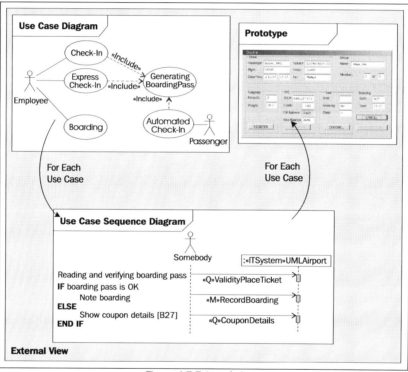

Figure 4.7 External view

The external view of the IT system consists of the following three elements:

- Use case diagrams show all users of the IT system (**actors**) and all tasks that users can perform with the IT system (**use cases**). In the following, we will generally talk about *a* use case diagram (singular). In practice it often makes little sense to depict all use cases of an IT system in a single diagram, as the diagram would be overcrowded.

- Use case sequence diagrams show the processes during interactions between user and IT system for individual use cases.

- Interface prototypes show how the user interface of a use case might look.

All three elements combined give a good overview over the IT system from a user perspective. In the following pages, we will discuss the elements individually.

4.1.3 Use Case Diagram

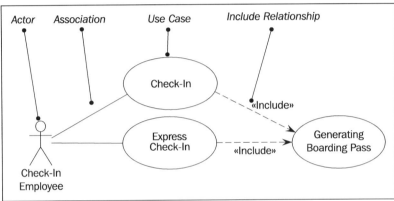

Figure 4.8 Elements of the use case diagram

In use case diagrams, as shown in Figure 4.8, we work with the following elements:

Actor

You can picture an actor as a user of the IT system, for example Mr. Steel or Mrs. Smith from check-in. Because individual persons are irrelevant for the model, they are abstracted. So the actors are called "check-in employee" or "passenger":

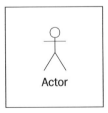

Actors represent roles that users take on when they use the IT system, e.g., the role of a check-in employee. One person can act in more than one role toward the IT system. It is important for the IT system in which role a person is acting. Therefore, it is necessary to log on to many IT systems in a certain role, for instance, as a normal user or as an administrator. In each case access to the appropriate functionalities (use cases) is granted.

Actors themselves are not part of the IT system. However, as employees they can be part of the business system (see Figure 4.5).

Use Case

Use cases describe the interactions that take place between actors and IT systems during the execution of business processes:

A use case represents a part of the functionality of the IT system and enables the user (modeled as an actor) to access this functionality.

Anything that users would like to do with the IT system has to be made available as a use case (or part of a use case). Functionalities that exist in the IT system, but that are not accessed by means of use cases, are *not* available to users.

Even though the idea behind use cases is to describe interactions, flows of batch processing, which generally do not include interactions, can also be described as use cases. The actor of such a batch use case is then the one who initiates batch processing. For instance, **generating check-in statistics** would be a batch use case.

Association

An association is a connection between an actor and a use case. An association indicates that an actor can carry out a use case. Several actors at one use case mean that each actor can carry out the use case on his or her own and not that the actors carry out the use case together:

According to UML, association only means that an actor is involved in a use case. We use associations in a restricted manner.

Include Relationships

An include relationship is a relationship between two use cases:

It indicates that the use case to which the arrow points is included in the use case on the other side of the arrow. This makes it possible to reuse a use case in another use case.

Figure 4.9 shows an example of this relationship. In the flow of the use case, express check-in is a point at which the use case generating boarding pass is included. This means that at this point the entire process generating boarding pass is carried out. Include relationships can be viewed as a type of call to a subprogram:

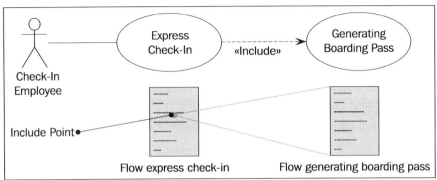

Figure 4.9 Include relationships between use cases

Reading Use Case Diagrams

Figure 4.10 shows a use case diagram with the actors (employee and passenger) as well as the use cases check-in and express check-in:

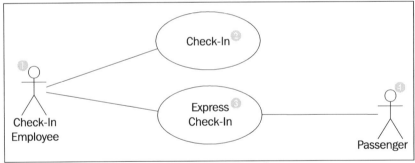

Figure 4.10 A simple use case diagram

According to your interest, you can start reading a use case diagram with the actor or with the use case.

Starting with the actor **check-in employee** (1) you can find associations between the two use cases **check-in** (2) and **express check-in** (3). This means that persons who interact with the IT system as check-in employees can carry out the use cases check-in and express check-in.

For the readability of the diagram it makes sense that use cases are located one below the other. However, this means nothing. A meaningful order in which a worker carries out use cases cannot be documented in a use case diagram.

Unless the use case diagram has to be amended, the use cases check-in (2) and express check-in (3) are everything that a check-in employee can do with the IT system. The actor passenger (5) has an association to the use case express check-in (3), which means that people who interact with the IT system as passengers can carry out the use case express check-in (3) directly with the IT system. The actor check-in employee (1) also has an association to the use case express check-in (3), which means that both passengers and check-in employees can carry out this use case. It does not mean that these two work together during express check-in.

Of course, during the use case check-in (2) too, a passenger checks himself or herself in and not an employee, but actor of the IT system is always the one who directly interacts with the IT system. For the use case express check-in (3) this can be either the passenger, who, with his or her plane ticket, can obtain a boarding pass at a machine, or a check-in employee who can do this in place of the passenger. However, for the business system the passenger is always the actor, because he or she is located outside the business. The employee, on the other hand, is not an actor from the perspective of the business system, because he or she works inside the business system.

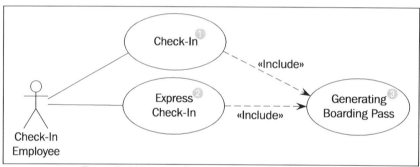

Figure 4.11 Use case diagram with include relationships

Figure 4.11 shows a use case diagram with the include relationships that both the use cases **check-in** (1) and **express check-in** (2) have with the use case **generating boarding pass** (3). This means that during both check-in and express check-in, a boarding pass is generated. According to our practical experience, this is the easiest way to reuse parts of use cases.

4.1.4 Query Events and Mutation Events

An event in UML is the specification of an occurrence: the description of something that happens. In the context of use cases, an event is something that a user does with the IT system. Events are initiated by users through the user interface, for instance, by clicking the Search button or pushing the Enter key. This has the effect that within the IT system something is processed. For us, it has proven valuable to differentiate between two types of events:

- **Query events** are events that have the goal of displaying information and usually don't change anything within the IT system. Query events result in displayed information.

- **Mutation events** are events that have the goal of storing, modifying, or deleting information in the IT system. The result of a mutation event depends on the success of the mutation: in the case of success information has been stored, modified, or deleted, which has to be conveyed to the user; in case of failure nothing has been changed, which also has to be conveyed to the user.

Since UML does not differentiate between query events and mutation events, we made use of UML extension stereotypes, which are a mechanism that allows the extension of UML with custom elements. We extended the language by creating two special cases of events:

- The stereotype «**Q**» in front of an event name indicates the special case of a query event.

- The stereotype «**M**» in front of an event name signifies the special case of a mutation event.

In this way, we can describe events in different diagram types, and make it immediately clear which type of event we are dealing with. Figure 4.12 shows query events and mutation events in a use case. The response of the IT system to the events is not depicted as a separate event. Each query and mutation event has implicit feedback: the obtained information, or a success or failure message:

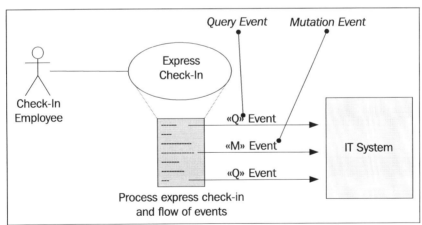

Figure 4.12 Query events «Q» and mutation events «M»

In the Hanseatic merchant's trading office we can picture the events as follows:

- Secretary Hildebrand finds out how much money the agent in Riga sent within the last six months. This is a **query event** «**Q**».

- Secretary Hildebrand summarizes the types and amounts of furs purchased from Russia up to this point. This is a **query event «Q»**.

- Secretary Hildebrand notes in the books that no further transactions should be conducted with the dyeing works of master Schildknecht. This is a **mutation event «M»**.

4.1.5 Use Case Sequence Diagram

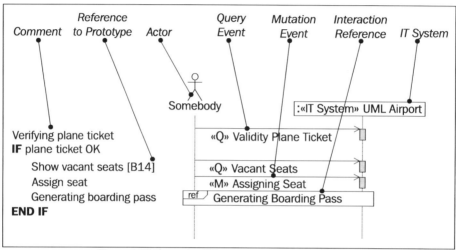

Figure 4.13 Elements of the use case sequence diagram

The use case sequence diagram is a special use of UML sequence diagrams that we advocate (see Figure 4.13). We will discuss the sequence diagram in detail in Section 4.4, *Interaction View*. In the use case sequence diagram, we work with the following elements:

Comment

The flow of the use case is described in a combination of textual description and sequence diagram:

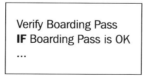

Comments can describe the flow of the use case in a simplistic manner; UML generally allows the placement of comments in all diagrams.

Reference to Prototype

References to screen forms, lists, and other elements of the user interface can be placed within comments:

This creates a link between the use case sequence diagram and the prototype.

Actor "Somebody"

Actor "somebody" represents any actor from the use case diagram. "Somebody" is the origin of all events within the use case that go to the IT system:

Because a use case can have different actors we use the actor "somebody". This way we don't have to specify a real actor.

Query Event

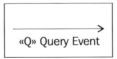

A query event is an event that is sent to the IT system with the goal of reading information (see Section 4.1.4, *Query Events and Mutation Events*).

Mutation Event

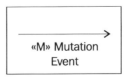

A mutation event is an event that is sent to the IT system with the goal of modifying information (again, see Section 4.1.4, *Query Events and Mutation Events*).

Interaction Reference

An interaction reference shows that at this point the use case sequence diagram of another use case is called (see the explanation of include relationships in Section 4.1.3, *Use Case Diagrams*).

IT System

The IT system represents the black box with all its objects and its entire functionality:

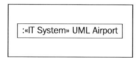

All events in the use case go to the IT system. In the external view we do not care which individual objects within the IT system are affected by the events.

Reading Use Case Sequence Diagrams

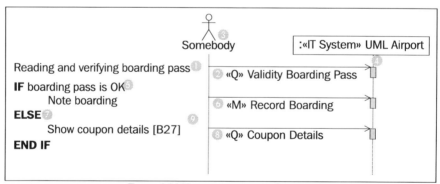

Figure 4.14 Use case sequence diagram

Figure 4.14 shows the use case sequence diagram of the use case **boarding**. A use case sequence diagram always belongs to a use case, because it describes the interaction flow of a use case. The flow becomes apparent from the comment at the left border. First, the boarding pass is read and verified (1) by sending the query event «**Q**» **validity boarding pass** (2) from the actor of the use case (3) to the IT system (4). How the event is treated internally cannot be seen in this diagram, because the IT system is viewed as a black box. The validity of the boarding pass is verified, which probably means that the information on the boarding pass that is read into the IT system is compared with the stored information. On the basis of the information that the IT system returns, users are able to see if the verification was successful or not. The result does not have its own arrow, but instead flows back through the query arrow (2).

If the boarding pass is OK (5), it can be recorded in the IT system that the passenger has boarded the plane. This happens through the mutation event «**M**» **record boarding** (6), which is sent to the IT system (4). Again, we cannot see what happens within the IT system. If the boarding pass is not OK (7), the display should show information about the ticket that belongs to this boarding pass. For this, again, a query event «**Q**» **coupon details** (8) coupon details, is sent to the IT system. This query results in the desired information, as long as it exists within the IT system. The display of information can be illustrated in an interface prototype. The reference [B27] (9) corresponds to a screen form in an interface prototype. Consequently, the entire use case **boarding** is described as a sequence of query and mutation events.

4.1.6 Constructing the External View

The following checklist shows the steps necessary to construct the external view. Subsequently, we will explain the individual steps further.

Checklist 4.1 Constructing Diagrams in the External View:

- Collect information sources—How am I supposed to know that?

- Identify potential actors—Who works with the IT system?

- Identify potential business use cases—What can be done with the IT system?

- Connect business use cases—Who can do what with the IT system?

- Describe actors—Who or what do the actors represent?

- Search for more business use cases—Which other functionalities does the IT system have to provide?

- Edit business use cases—What actually has to be included in a business use case?

- Document business use cases—What happens in a business use case?

- Model relationships between business use cases—What can be reused?

- Verify the view—Is everything correct?

The order in which these steps are given makes sense. However, this order is not mandatory, since in practice, the individual steps often overlap heavily.

Normally, these steps will be carried out by an analyst, who needs to have a general understanding of the IT system as well as of the business system as it was modeled in Chapter 3, *Modeling Business Systems*. However, it is indispensable to consult additional knowledge carriers, such as users of the system. The result of these work steps is the external view, which has to be read and understood by domain experts.

Collect Information Sources—How Am I Supposed to Know That?

Generally, there are quite a number of information sources that can be used for the formulation of the external view:

- Certainly, the business system model is the first source that should be drawn upon. The business system's actors, workers, and use cases are a good starting point from which it is possible to derive actors and use cases of the IT system (see Chapter 3, *Modeling Business Systems*).
- Technical specifications, project specifications, and similar documents.
- Future users are a very important source for this user-oriented external view.
- Technical experts in the IT system's area of application.
- Organization charts, organizational structure, and job descriptions.

Taking up the users' standpoint is very helpful. Talk with users or observe them performing their jobs.

Identify Potential Actors—Who Works with the IT System?

This step is about identifying a first selection of actors. This selection does not yet have to be complete or correct. The rule applies: the more, the better. You can continue working with these actors in subsequent steps.

Answering the following questions (for instance, with users of the system) will help identify potential actors. While doing this, you should try to abstain from using persons mentioned by name. Instead, try to form groups of people or actors:

- Which actors and employees of the business system deal directly with the IT system?
- Which groups of people need support from the IT system in order to complete their daily work?
- Which groups of people perform the most important main functions of the IT system?

- Which groups of people are needed to carry out secondary system functions, such as maintenance and administration?
- Which groups of people from the organization model (see organization chart) of the company or division work with the IT system?

Here, it is important to picture concrete and direct interactions with the IT system under consideration.

At a check-in counter it is the check-in employee who is in direct interaction with the IT system. At the check-in machine, where passengers without luggage can check in with their machine-readable tickets, it is the passenger who directly interacts with the IT system, inserting the ticket and choosing one of the empty seats.

A passenger is also an actor in the business system; check-in employees and boarding employees, on the other hand, are not. They are employees, and because of that, they are part of the business system, as shown in Figure 4.15:

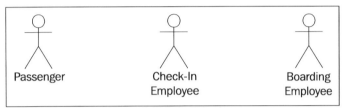

Figure 4.15 Potential actors

Identify Potential Use Cases—What Can be Done With the IT System?

This step is about finding a first selection of use cases. Here too, the rule applies: the more, the better. Answering the following questions will help identify potential use cases:

- Which business use cases of the business system are supported by the IT system?
- Which business activities of the business system should be supported by the IT system?
- Depending on the degree of detail of the business activities, in this step a use case can be constructed for each business activity.
- What are the goal and purpose of the IT system?
- What are the main functions of the IT system?
- For what do actors need the IT system?

- Which secondary system functions, such as maintenance and administration, does the IT system require?
- What functions does the interface prototype have?

Figure 4.16 Potential use cases

Connect Actors and Use Cases—Who Can Do What with the IT System?

Assigning business use cases to actors generates a first draft of the use case diagram, as shown in Figure 4.16. Here, the following question should be answered:

- Which actor can carry out which use cases?

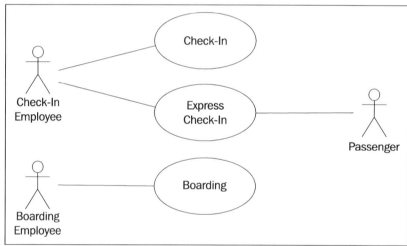

Figure 4.17 First draft of a use case diagram

This first draft constitutes a foundation from which the use case diagram can be edited and refined, as shown in Figure 4.17.

Describe Actors—Who or What do the Actors Represent?

An actor in a diagram has to be named (or renamed) in a way that clarifies the role that is represented. The question is:

- How can an actor be accurately described? Here it is extremely important that the terminology of the domain is used. Users of the IT system have to recognize themselves in the actors; otherwise they will not understand the use case diagram! If required, the actor can be defined with a comment in addition to an accurate name. Such a comment can include the field of responsibility of the actor, the requirements of the IT system from the actor's perspective, or a formal definition of the role that the actor plays.

Search for More Use Cases—What Functionalities does the IT System have to Provide?

Once you have identified a first selection of use cases, these can be used as the starting point for the completion of the use case diagram. Use cases that were overlooked before can be identified by asking the following questions, based on a particular use case:

- Is there anything that has to be done with the IT system at some point before a particular use case can be executed?
- Is there anything that has to be done with the IT system at some point after a particular use case is executed?
- Is there anything that has to be done with the IT system if it does not execute a particular use case?

It is very important not to lose sight of the real IT system. There is a risk of modeling use cases that lie outside the IT system under consideration. For example, purchasing the plane ticket, which has to occur before check-in, does not belong to the considered IT system passenger services.

In our case study, the answers for the use case check-in could be as follows:

- Information about ticket and flight has to be obtained before check-in.
- Boarding has to take place after check-in.
- The plane ticket has to be invalidated if the passenger does not appear at check-in.

Edit Use Cases—What Actually Has to be Included in a Use Case?

The most difficult part of modeling use cases probably is finding the appropriate degree of detail for these use cases. Here, the range is between the two extremes shown in Figure 4.18:

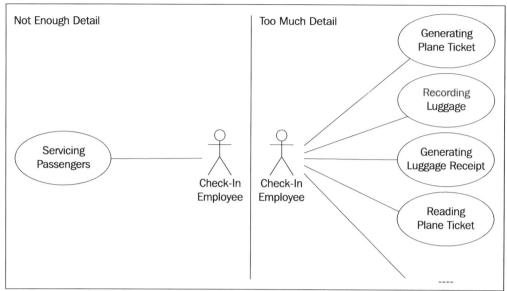

Figure 4.18 Extreme degrees of detail in the IT system "Passenger Services"

Neither approach makes sense. If the entire IT system is crammed into one use case, a practically meaningless use case diagram is constructed. Nothing useful can be learned from it. If on the other hand, use cases are itemized too strongly, the use case diagram gets too complex and contains too many use cases with interrelationships that are hard to recognize.

Fortunately, there are some criteria that will help you find the optimal scope of a use case. To prevent use cases from becoming too large, we can ask the following questions for each use case:

- Does the use case consist of a behaviorally related sequence of interactions that belong together (an interaction sequence)? Items that are included in a business use case have to be directly related. Issuing a boarding pass and searching for lost luggage are not related at all. Use cases that violate this criterion have to be divided.

- Can a single actor carry out the use case? Even though UML allows more than one actor to be involved in the execution of a use case, in most cases, it is better to abstain from this option. If a use case describes the interaction of a person with a computer, it implies that not more than one person should be involved in the interaction. Use cases that violate this criterion have to be divided.

To avoid the creation of use cases that are too small, we can ask the following questions for each use case:

- Does the use case deliver a tangible and relevant result? A use case cannot describe an incomplete sub-step by itself, such as *choose customer*. Rather, a use case has to produce a result that makes sense from a domain point of view. Use cases that violate this criterion have to be combined with other use cases.

- Is the use case never performed alone, but always in a sequence in combination with other business use cases? Use cases are not supposed to describe sub-steps that are only executed in combination with other sub-steps. Use cases that violate this criterion have to be combined with other use cases.

Verifying existing use cases with these questions can help finding a meaningful degree of detail by dividing or combining use cases.

Document Use Cases—What Happens in a Use Case?

The information from the use case diagram is not sufficient to understand use cases. The flow of interaction that stands behind a use case has to be described. In addition to purely verbal description, description in a use case sequence diagram has proven to be especially valuable. We can ask the following questions when developing a use case sequence diagram for the use case:

- What steps are involved in working with the IT system? To answer this question we have to observe the actor's work with the IT system. What does the actor do with the IT system? What does he or she enter? What does the IT system display? What does the interaction look like? Here, it is important to find the appropriate level of detail. Not every key pressed makes up a work step. The next two questions will help you find the appropriate level of detail.

- Which information is the use case meant to provide to the actor? If information should be displayed, a query event is sent to the IT system.

- Which information is meant to be stored, modified, or deleted in the IT system? If information should be changed, a mutation event is sent to the IT system.

The description of the flow is, therefore, a succession of steps in which information is entered or queried, in other words, an interaction. During the description of the flow, the IT system is always viewed as a black box.

Because, in reality, a use case does not always take place in the same manner, it has proven valuable to use simple control structures in descriptions to show alternatives and branches, as illustrated in Figure 4.19:

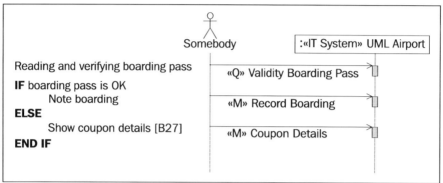

Figure 4.19 Use case sequence diagram for the use case "Boarding"

The documentation of use cases should also include a description of the user interface utilized. An example of this is the dialogue window labeled [B27] above, shown in Figure 4.20:

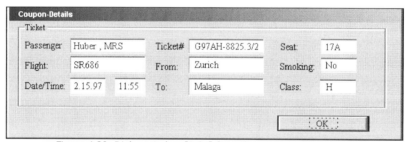

Figure 4.20: Dialog window [B 27] from the use case "Boarding"

Model Relationships between Use Cases—What can be Reused?

If you notice that certain parts of the interaction are the same in several use cases, these commonalities can be included into their own use case. With an include relationship this new use case can be utilized in other use cases. The question for this is:

- Are there parts or sections that exist in several use case sequence diagrams (and always remain the same)?

Verify the View—Is Everything Correct?

Use case diagrams, as well as use case sequence diagrams, have to be verified with the aid of knowledge carriers. Ideally, knowledge carriers can read and understand the diagrams themselves (which is not that difficult, since our book has reading instructions for every view). Then, the knowledge carriers are in a position to answer the question about completeness and correctness themselves. If this is not possible, the diagrams have to be read to the knowledge carriers. Then, the diagrams have to be verified for correctness and completeness jointly. Only with this last step is the circle complete and a verified view that reflects a current shared understanding of the IT system created.

The completed use case diagram can be verified with the following checklist:

Checklist 4.2 Verifying Use Case Diagrams in the External View:

- Is the use case diagram complete? The use case diagram is complete if there are no further use cases. Anything that users have to do with the IT system is depicted in the form of use cases (if necessary, use cases can be spread out into several diagrams).

- Are all use cases correct? Use cases are correct if they describe a use case of the IT system and comply with the definition of a use case.

- Is the degree of detail appropriate? The degree of detail of the business use cases should meet the following requirements:

  A use case represents a behaviorally coherent interaction sequence.

  A use case is carried out by a single actor.

  A use case represents a functionality that is tangible and that yields a relevant result.

- Generally, a use case is carried out completely.

- Are the use cases named appropriately? The name of each use case should describe the activity that is executed in the IT system.

- Are the actors correct? The actors in the use case diagram represent roles that someone (e.g., a person) or something (e.g., another system) takes up in an interaction with the IT system.

Completed use case sequence diagrams can be verified with the following checklist:

Checklist 4.3 Verifying Use Case Sequence Diagrams in the External View:

- Are the use case sequence diagrams completely present? Every use case should have a sequence diagram that describes the possible flows of the use case.

- Are the use case sequence diagrams correct? Each use case sequence diagram should contain only one object that represents the IT system and be made up exclusively of query events and mutation events.

4.2 Structural View

4.2.1 Objects and Classes

The basis of the object-oriented approach is as good as possible a representation of something that exists in the real world first in a model and later in an IT system. However, this representation will never completely correspond to reality. Everything in the real world, whether it is a living being, an object, or an idea, is so complex and has so many aspects, that this complexity can never be completely represented:

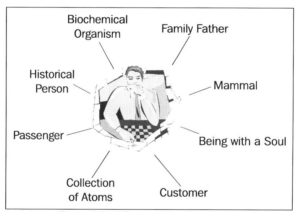

Figure 4.21 A few aspects of Mr. Smith

To allow representation as a model it is necessary to focus on a few particular aspects and to leave out all others. The essential, meaning the interesting, aspects are emphasized and all other aspects are omitted. It is exactly this that is the art of modeling objects.

In order to model objects successfully we have to know for what purpose they are needed in the IT system. The object "Mr. Smith" will look different in a customer management system than in a medical information system or in a tax register (see Figure 4.21). Only when we know, at least approximately, the purpose of the IT system we can build functional objects.

In models, we always abstract from reality in a target-oriented manner. We restrict our consideration to the important aspects for the current purpose and omit everything else. Figure 4.22 shows this step of abstraction by the example of an airplane:

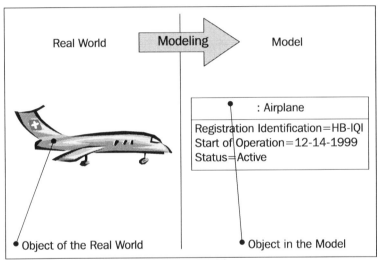

Figure 4.22 Modeling

When depicting the real world in abstract models, we differentiate between two steps. In the first step, we abstract from individual persons or things to objects. In the second step, we combine similar objects into classes. Figure 4.23 shows, with a few examples, how things of the real world are depicted first as objects and then as classes:

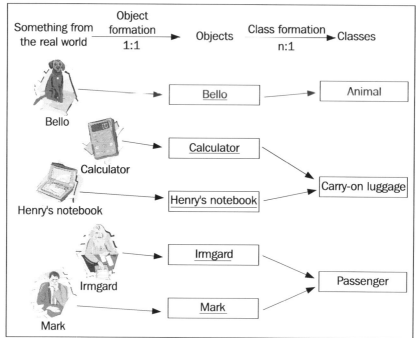

Figure 4.23 Object and Class formation

The direct illustration in a model of something that exists in the real world leads to an object. A 1:1 relationship exists between something from the real world and the object. The object represents exactly one particular exemplar from the real world. In a database an object corresponds, for instance, to an entry in a spreadsheet. The definition of objects is already a first step of abstraction, since only relevant features are modeled in the object. For example, in the object Mark, the person Mark is reduced to those aspects that are important for a passenger, for instance, title, first name, last name, and date of birth.

> Write down a dozen objects from your personal work environment.

In the second step of abstraction, we combine similar objects into classes. **Similar** means:

- That the goal of the abstraction is similar
- That we are interested in similar characteristics
- That the objects have similar behavior

Most of the time the two steps of abstraction are combined, meaning that classes are formed directly. The step of object creation is not carried out explicitly.

Modeling is often made more difficult by the fact that something that only exists as a concept or idea, and not in the physical sense, has to be modeled. While in the past it was still possible to actually hold a stock certificate or a savings book in your hands, today, such things often exist only as information.

Try to group the objects that you wrote down into classes.

Dealing with classes becomes easier when you consider that the term class has two somewhat different meanings:

- On the one hand, the class is the **pattern** according to which objects are created.

- On the other hand, the class is the **set of objects** that have been created according to that class.

The class as a pattern dictates the characteristics and behavior of objects that are created from the class. In Figure 4.24, class is compared with a cookie cutter, which can be used to cut cookies (objects of the class) from dough:

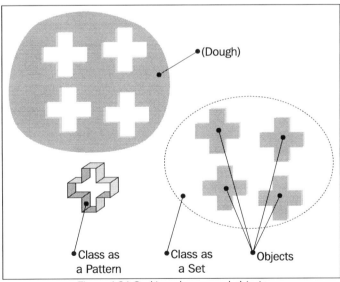

Figure 4.24 Cookies, classes, and objects

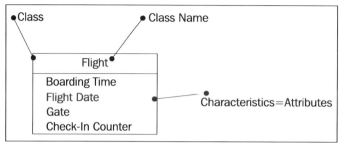

Figure 4.25 Class as a pattern

The class as a set contains and knows all its objects. It can be pictured as a table in a database, which knows all its entries.

Usually, classes, in addition to attributes, contain methods, which specify the behavior of objects. However, in our approach to modeling IT systems we broadly abstain from using this possibility. The behavior of objects depends largely on their respective states. A "cancel flight" method of the class "flight", for instance, has to perform something different with a flight object in the condition "in execution" than with a flight object in the condition "planned".

According to our experience, such rules can generally be modeled much more easily in the statechart diagram in the behavioral view than they can be modeled with operations. Only in the later project stages of design and implementation is the behavior of classes converted into methods according to the programming language utilized.

In the Hanseatic merchant's trading office a class corresponds to a book, for example a customer index, and the clerk who is responsible for the book. The book can only be accessed through the clerk. Individual customer entries correspond to the objects. Entries in the different books are connected by cross-references.

4.2.2 Generalization, Specialization, and Inheritance

Terms such as superclass, subclass, or inheritance come to mind when thinking about the object-oriented approach. These concepts are very important when dealing with object-oriented programming languages such as Java, Smalltalk, or C++. For modeling classes that illustrate technical concepts they are secondary. The reason for this is that modeling relevant objects or ideas from the real world gives little opportunity for using inheritance (compare the class diagram of our case study). Nevertheless, we would like to further introduce these terms at this point in Figure 4.26:

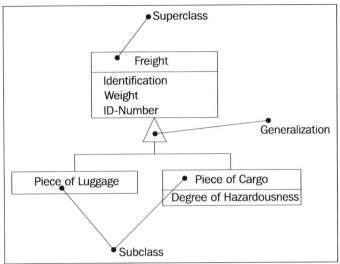

Figure 4.26 Notation of generalization

Generalization is the process of extracting shared characteristics from two or more classes, and combining them into a generalized superclass. Shared characteristics can be attributes, associations, or methods.

In Figure 4.27, the classes **Piece of Luggage** (1) and **Piece of Cargo** (2) partially share the same attributes. From a domain perspective, the two classes are also very similar. During generalization, the shared characteristics (3) are combined and used to create a new superclass **Freight** (4). **Piece of Luggage** (5) and **Piece of Cargo** (6) become subclasses of the class **Freight**.

The shared attributes (3) are only listed in the superclass, but also apply to the two subclasses, even though they are not listed there.

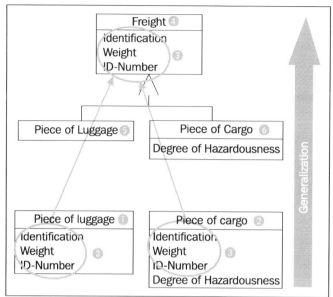

Figure 4.27 Example of generalization

Consider whether some of the classes that you found could be generalized.

In contrast to generalization, **specialization** means creating new subclasses from an existing class. If it turns out that certain attributes, associations, or methods only apply to some of the objects of the class, a subclass can be created. The most inclusive class in a generalization/specialization is called the superclass and is generally located at the top of the diagram. The more specific classes are called subclasses and are generally placed below the superclass.

In Figure 4.28, the class **Freight** (1) has the attribute **Degree of Hazardousness** (2), which is needed only for cargo, but not for passenger luggage. Additionally (not visible in Figure 4.28), only passenger luggage has a connection to a coupon. Obviously, here two similar but different domain concepts are combined into one class. Through specialization the two special cases of freights are formed: **Piece of Cargo** (3) and **Piece of Luggage** (4). The attribute **Degree of Hazardousness** (5) is placed where it belongs—in **Piece of Cargo**. The attributes of the class **Freight** (1) also apply to the two subclasses **Piece of Cargo** (3) and **Piece of Luggage** (4):

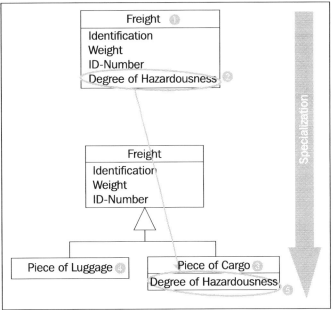

Figure 4.28 Example of specialization

Consider whether some of the classes that you found could be specialized.

So much for the mechanism. However, the domain meaning of the relationship between superclass and subclass is much more important. These rules apply to this relationship:

- All statements that are made about a superclass also apply to all subclasses. We say that subclasses "**inherit**" attributes, associations, and operations from the superclass. For example: If the superclass **Freight** has an attribute **Weight**, then the subclass piece of luggage also has an attribute Weight, even though this attribute is not listed in the subclass **Piece of Luggage**.

- Anything that can be done with an object of the superclass can also be done with an object of the subclass. For example: If freight can be loaded, pieces of luggage can also be loaded.

- In the terminology of the system that is being modeled, a subclass has to be a special form of the superclass. For example: A piece of luggage is a special case of freight. The counter-example to this is: A flight is not a special case of a flight number.

4.2.3 Static and Dynamic Business Rules

Business rules are domain rules that are depicted in an IT system model. Domain rules can be derived from business strategies, requirements, technical guidelines, and restrictions. Business rules are unrelated to information technology; they are purely derived from the domain. Examples of business rules are:

- During check-in, each passenger has to be assigned a seat.
- For each flight, each seat can only be assigned to one passenger.
- A flight cannot be canceled once it has been started.

Many requirements cannot be modeled as business rules. In addition to the IT system model, a requirement catalog is part of specifying an IT system. We do not further address requirement catalogs in this text.

Business rules can be divided into two categories:

- **Static business rules**: Business rules that can be verified at any point in time. These business rules deal with the static structures of classes. These business rules can be documented in class diagrams of the structural view.

- **Dynamic business rules**: Business rules that can only be verified at a certain point in time, namely, when something happens. These business rules deal with the dynamic behavior of the objects of a class. These business rules can be documented in the statechart diagram of the behavioral view.

4.2.4 Elements of the View

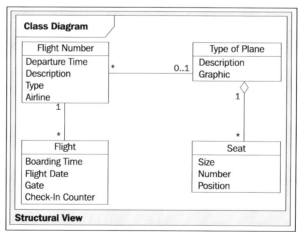

Figure 4.29 Structural view

The structural view of IT systems, as shown in Figure 4.29, consists of one or several class diagrams. Class diagrams show all relevant classes of the IT system, their relationships to each other (associations), their characteristics (attributes), and in basic terms, their behavior (methods). It is the best-known view of the object-oriented approach, and unfortunately, often the only diagram that is constructed. Class diagrams show the internal static structures of the IT system.

4.2.5 Class Diagram

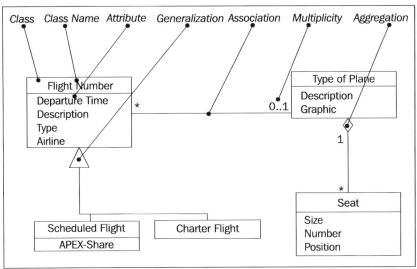

Figure 4.30 Elements of the class diagram

In class diagrams, as shown in Figure 4.30, we work with the following elements:

Class

A class represents a relevant concept from the domain, a set of persons, objects, or ideas that are depicted in the IT system:

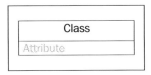

Examples of classes are passengers, planes, or tickets.

Attribute

An attribute of a class represents a characteristic of a class that is of interest for the user of the IT system:

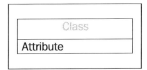

Characteristics of interest of a passenger, for example, are name and age.

Generalization

Generalization is a relationship between two classes: a general class and a special class:

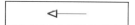

Refer to Section 4.2.2, *Generalization, Specialization, and Inheritance.*

Association

An association represents a relationship between two classes:

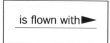

An association indicates that objects of one class have a relationship with objects of another class, in which this connection has a specifically defined meaning (for example, "is flown with").

Multiplicity

A multiplicity allows for statements about the number of objects that are involved in an association:

Also see Figure 4.32.

Aggregation

An aggregation is a special case of an association (see above) meaning "consists of":

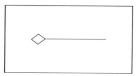

The diamond documents this meaning; a caption is unnecessary.

Reading Class Diagrams

Figure 4.31 shows a class diagram from our case study with the classes customer, ticket, and coupon, their attributes, and their associations:

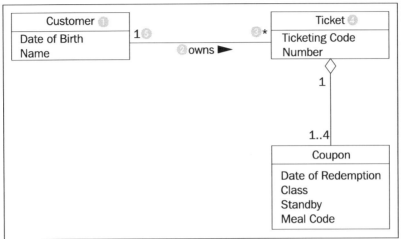

Figure 4.31 Class diagram with associations

Looking at the class diagram in Figure 4.31, you can read the association between the classes customer and ticket as follows:

- One (this sentence always begins with "one") object of the first class has an association with a number of objects of the second class.

The appropriate values from the diagram have to be inserted into this first abstract formulation, which can be universally applied. The name of one class is customer (1); the name of the other class is ticket (4). The name of the association is owns (2):

- A customer (1) owns (2) * (3) ticket (4).

If the asterisk is exchanged with its meaning, a regular English sentence is created:

- A customer (1) owns (2) zero, one or several (3) ticket(s) (4).

Since associations usually are not directional, meaning usually go both directions, our association also has a meaning in the other direction:

- A ticket (4) is owned by (2) exactly one (5) customer (1).

The small triangle next to the name of the association (2) indicates in which direction the name of the association holds true.

We can read all the associations in the class diagram in this way.

The specification of the number of objects of the second class (you always start with one object of the first class) is called the multiplicity. The course of action should always be according to the same pattern:

First, a statement of the lower limit (minimum number) followed by two periods (..) and a statement of the upper limit (maximum number).

Figure 4.32 shows the most common possibilities:

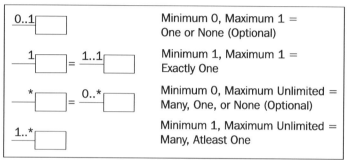

Figure 4.32 Multiplicities

However, in UML it is also possible to insert any values as the lower and upper limits, e.g., 2 .. 4 or 6 .. *.

The association's name is necessary for understanding the domain meaning of the association. In contrast to the association itself, which applies to both directions, the name of the association applies to only one direction, which is indicated by a black triangle. If the association is not labeled, its meaning has to be derived from the domain context, or it takes on a general meaning such as has or belongs to. In case of doubt it is better to label associations too much than too little. Many diagrams that we have encountered in our practical experience were incomprehensible because associations were not labeled.

Associations can also be viewed as the implementation of static business rules (see Section 4.2.3, *Static and Dynamic Business Rules*). Statements such as "a ticket belongs to exactly one customer" are documented in the class diagram by associations.

Roles are another possible way in UML to give relationships between classes a domain meaning. In this way, we can state what role an object of one class plays for the objects of another class:

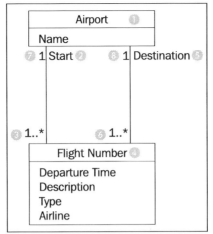

Figure 4.33 Class diagram with roles

Looking at the class diagram in Figure 4.33, we can read the left association with roles between the classes flight number and airport as follows:

- An **airport** (1) is a **start (location)** (2) for **one** or **more** (3) **flight numbers** (4).

There is another association between the two classes flight number and airport:

- An airport (1) is a destination (5) for one or more flight numbers (4).

These two associations also have inversions, even though roles are only stated for one direction:

- A **flight number** (4) has as **start (location)** (2) **exactly one** (7) **airport** (1).
- A flight number (4) has as destination (5) exactly one (8) airport (1).

This records that a certain flight number has a departure airport and a destination airport. An example of a flight number is LX317, a daily flight of the Swiss airline Crossair from London to Zurich.

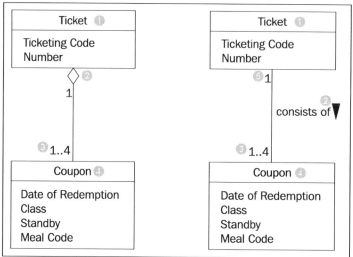

Figure 4.34 Class diagram with Aggregation

Among the many domain meanings that an association can have there is one that can be signified with UML by its own symbol: the whole-part relationship or aggregation. This type of relationship is always used when objects of one class are a part of objects of another class.

In the class diagram in Figure 4.34 aggregation is used on the left side (the white diamond), which can be read as follows:

- A ticket (1) consists of (2) 1 to 4 (3) coupons (4).

or the other way around:

- A coupon (4) is part of (2) exactly one (5) ticket (1).

The example without a diamond, but with a name for the association, has exactly the same meaning! The last missing element of UML that we use to model class diagrams is generalization/specialization, which serves to depict the relationship between a superclass and a subclass. The generalization/specialization in Figure 4.35 can be read from top to bottom or bottom to top. If you begin at the top, you find a class **Freight** (1) with the attributes: Identification, Weight, and ID-number (2). This class has two specializations, **Piece of Luggage** (3) and **Piece of Cargo** (4). The class Piece of Cargo has an additional attribute: Degree of Hazardousness (5).

If you begin at the bottom you will find the classes Piece of Luggage (3) and Piece of Cargo (4). These have a superclass, the class Freight (1), which contains the shared attributes (and functions) of the subclasses.

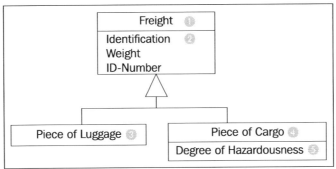

Figure 4.35 Class diagram with generalization/specialization

4.2.6 Constructing Class Diagrams

The main problem for constructing class diagrams is finding the "right" classes. We address this problem from two perspectives and construct the class diagram in two work steps.

In top-down analysis, classes are found first on the basis of general understanding of the subject matter. Top-down analysis is about finding a basic structure of classes that the bottom-up analysis, which is more detailed, can build upon. The (simplified) question is:

- Which information or domain concepts can be of use for my IT system?

Domain knowledge, verbal descriptions of the area of application, and user representatives are important sources of information. In this way, a basic structure of classes can be found for most IT systems.

In bottom-up analysis, classes are found mainly on the basis of the inputs and outputs of the IT system. The question is:

- What information is needed for the individual inputs and outputs of the IT system?

Here, the classes that were found during top-down analysis serve as the basis to find these classes. Already existing inputs and outputs, for instance, screen forms and paper forms are important sources of information.

According to our experience, these two work steps lead to good results in modeling IT systems that manage lots of information. In contrast to this, there are systems that, for example, have the function of running or controlling something, which have a complex functionality but hardly manage any data. For such systems we recommend a less data-intensive approach, for instance, responsibility-driven design. (For this approach compare *Rebecca Wirfs-Brock, Brian Wilkerson, Lauren Wiener: Designing Object-Oriented Software, Prentice Hall 1998.*)

The following checklist shows the necessary steps for constructing class diagrams. Subsequently, we will explain the individual steps further.

Checklist 4.4 Constructing Class Diagrams in the Structural View:

Top-down Analysis

- Identify and model classes—Which classes do we need?

- Identify and model associations—How are the classes connected?

- Define attributes—What do we want to know about the objects?

Bottom-up Analysis

- List required queries and inputs—What does the IT system need to deliver and accept?

- Formulate queries and inputs—How exactly should the display look?

- Conduct information analysis—Which classes, associations, and attributes do we need?

- Consolidate class diagrams—How does everything fit together?

- Verify the class diagrams—Is everything correct?

Identify and Model Classes—Which Classes do We Need?

An analysis of the interrelationships, information needs, and actors and prototypes is conducted on the basis of general domain knowledge, discussions with experts, and documents. The questions that should be asked are:

- What are the most important things that will be worked with in the IT system?
- What classes can be created from this?

The answers to these questions provide a number of potential classes, which we model in a first draft of the class diagram. In practice, the results of this first work step vary greatly. However, we have never experienced a case in which nothing at all was found. If you are still inexperienced in identifying classes, it has proven helpful to run through top-down analysis repeatedly. With time, you will develop a sense for what is a class and what is not (Figure 4.36):

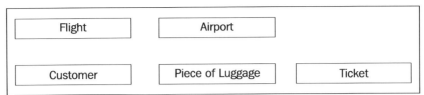

Figure 4.36 Potential classes

Identify and Model Associations—How Are the Classes Connected?

We model the interconnections between the obtained classes and business rules in class diagrams as associations with meaningful names and multiplicities, as shown in Figure 4.37. The questions are:

- What relationships exist among objects?
- How many objects of each class are involved in a relationship?

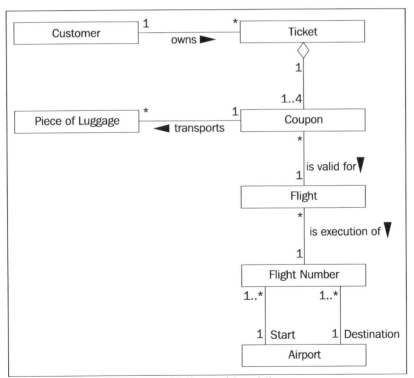

Figure 4.37 Class and Associations

The first question has to be asked for objects of each pair of different classes, for instance, for the classes flight and customer from our case study. Here, it is important to recognize whether the relationship is direct, or if the relationship only exists indirectly through other objects. In our example it turns out that a customer owns a ticket, which in turn, consists of coupons, which are valid for a flight. The goal of the second question is to determine the multiplicity of the relationship, for instance, how many tickets a customer can have, and to how many customers a ticket belongs (Figure 4.37).

Even though at the beginning of this work step we started with previously found classes, because of the domain discussions, we generally find more classes in this work step.

Define Attributes—What do We Want to Know about the Objects?

The required information about a class has to be identified and modeled in the form of attributes. The question for this is:

- Which information about a certain class am I interested in?

This question is about finding obviously needed attributes of the individual classes (see Figure 4.38). This question cannot be answered completely without precisely analyzing inputs and queries, as takes place in bottom-up analysis. Because of this, not too much time should be spent answering this question.

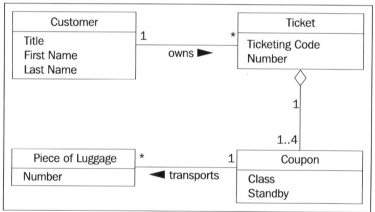

Figure 4.38 Classes and Attributes

List Required Queries and Inputs—What does the IT System Need to Deliver and Accept?

In this first work step of bottom-up analysis, the individual queries and inputs of the IT system have to be identified. The queries are more important here, because answering queries is the real purpose of IT systems. The questions are:

- What information does the IT system have to be able to provide?
- What information does the IT system have to be able to accept?

When answering these questions, you can build upon the use cases already found. Which queries and mutations occur in a use case is already drafted in the use case sequence diagram. Another source of information are the business processes of the business system (see Chapter 3, *Modeling Business Systems*). The result of this work step is a list of information requirements, as illustrated in Figure 4.39:

Requirements	Type	Use Case
Boarding Pass	Output	Generating Boarding Pass
Passenger List	Output	Complete Boarding
Ticket Details	Output	Check-In, Express Check-In
Customer Details	Output	Check-In, Express Check-In
Coupon	Input	Check-In, Express Check-In
...		

Figure 4.39 List of information requirements

Formulate Queries and Inputs—How Exactly Should the Display Look?

In order to create individual class diagrams for the individual queries and inputs, we first need to be define how they look. Complex query results or inputs are collected or drafted. Figure 4.40 shows a passenger list; further examples can be found in Figure 4.66 (display) and Figure 4.67 (boarding pass). The question is:

- How precisely does the display of a query or input look?

Good sources of information are already existing forms (for example, the passenger list from Figure 4.40) and displays from the prototypes:

Passenger List for Flight LX317
of 4.9.2003, Stand 08:10 hr

Mr	Shirodkar	Abhishek
Mr	Adams	Douglas
Ms	Sakpal	Shilpa
Mr	Baumann	Philippe
Mr	Mohite	Nilesh
Mr	Cleese	John
Ms	Padmanabhan	Nanda
Mr	Jahagirdar	Niranjan
Ms	Chakrabarti	Paramita
Mr	Jarchow	Thomas
Mr	Kamal	Jone
Mr	Gubser	Rolf
Mr	Smith	Harry
Mr	Pande	Ashutosh
Mr	Milligan	Spike
Mr	Schacher	Mark
Mr	Kandalgaonkar	Dinesh

Side 1

Figure 4.40 Passenger list

Conduct Information Analysis—Which Classes, Associations, and Attributes Do We Need?

In this work step the main part of the bottom-up analysis is performed. For each query or input a small class diagram is created on the basis of the existing classes. This is achieved by modeling the drafted inputs and outputs of the IT system. Class modeling on a small scale takes place. The questions are:

- What data elements exist in input and output?
- What objects hide behind these data elements?
- What relationships exist between the objects that were found?
- Which of the objects that have already been modeled can be used?

For the passenger list in Figure 4.40, the class diagram in Figure 4.41 can be constructed:

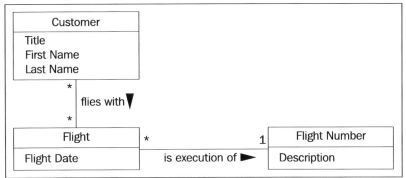

Figure 4.41 Class diagram for the passenger list

Taking into consideration the classes that were already found in the top-down analysis, the class diagram in Figure 4.42 is constructed:

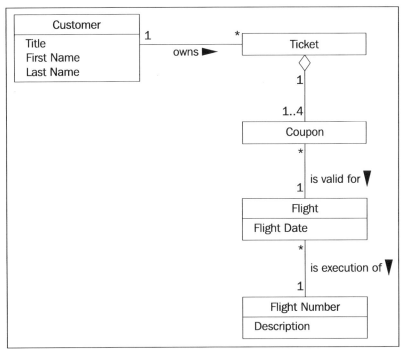

Figure 4.42 Edited class diagram for passenger list

Consolidate Class Diagrams—How Does Everything Fit Together?

In this last work step, if it has not been done yet, the individual class diagrams have to be consolidated into one cumulative class diagram. Here, inconsistencies have to be discovered and corrected. Applicable questions are:

- Are there classes in the individual class diagrams that have different names, but represent the same thing?

- Are there multiple relationships in individual class diagrams that have the same meaning?

- Are there attributes within classes that are named differently, but that have the same meaning?

In fact, when all individual class diagrams are being consolidated to one cumulative diagram, these questions almost pose themselves. Once inconsistencies have been recognized, they can usually be corrected easily. If you used the classes found during top-down analysis for modeling the drafted inputs and outputs, overlaps and conflicts during the consolidation of the individual class diagrams should be limited anyway.

Verify the Class Diagrams—Is Everything Correct?

The completed class diagram in the structural view can be verified with the following checklist:

Checklist 4.5 Verifying Class Diagrams of the Structural View:

- Is the class diagram complete? This question will be answered in Section 4.4, *Interaction View*. In the interaction view, we will show how the class diagram can be used to answer all required queries of the IT system. If this is possible, the class diagram is complete.

- Is the class diagram correct? The second question, the question about correctness, is a little bit more difficult to answer. Our experience shows that intensive collaborative reading of class diagrams together with the knowledge carriers will bring to light most mistakes. In addition to that, the class diagram can be tested for suspect structure patterns. The best way to do this is with a suitable tool. An introduction to the analysis of structure patterns would go beyond the scope of the text. An explanation of concepts and of a tool that helps analyze structure patterns can be found at http://www.knowgravity.com/eng/value/cassandra.htm.

4.3 The Behavioral View

4.3.1 The Life of an Object

Persons, objects, or concepts from the real world, which we model as objects in the IT system, have "lives". Actually, they have two lives; the original in the real world has a life, and our image, the object, has a life as well. Though these two lives are related, they do not necessarily follow the same course. Usually, a life starts at birth, creation, or generation and ends with death, deletion, or destruction. In between, life follows a more or less ordered course, as illustrated in Figure 4.43:

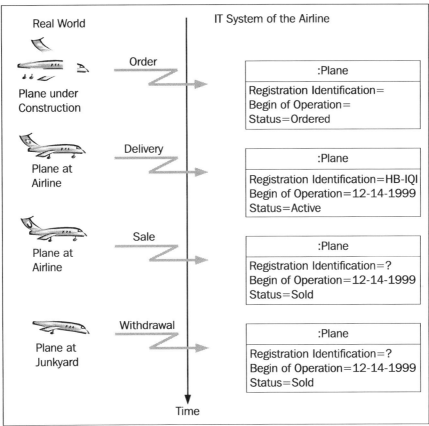

Figure 4.43 The life of a plane

To illustrate what we mentioned before we would like to take a closer look at the life of a plane. The plane that we would like to look at is an Airbus A330-223 of Swiss International Airlines with the registration number HB-IQI.

- The birth of the Airbus A330-223 (of the **original**) occurs, depending on the perspective, at the start of construction or at the first flight.

- The birth of the **object** of the Airbus A330-223 in the IT system occurs when information about the plane is recorded for the first time. This can be at the point of purchase, since the plane could be recorded in the IT system for planning purposes, or when the plane is delivered. The initiator for the birth of an object in the IT system is always a mutation event.

Because commercial airplanes are often sold long before construction begins, it is possible that the birth of the object occurs before the (physical) birth of the plane.

- The death of the **original** has to do with physical destruction. In the case of our Airbus A330-233 death occurs at withdrawal or possibly in a plane crash.

- The death of the **object** occurs, when the object is deleted from the IT system of Swiss Airline. The initiator for the death of an object in the IT system is always a mutation event.

Because commercial airplanes are often sold on after a certain period of time, it is possible that the (logical) death of an object in the IT system occurs before the (physical) death of the original.

Between birth and death the object is alive in the IT system, that is, it will be read and changed. It will be read as the result of a query event; it will be changed as the result of a mutation event (see Section 4.1.4, *Query Events and Mutation Events*).

As long as reading and modifying objects are not subject to any restrictions, this is not especially interesting. It can be described in a simple statechart diagram (see Figure 4.44). However, as soon as rules for modification have to be observed, it becomes important to document these rules somewhere. Here, we are talking about dynamic business rules (see Section 4.2.3, *Static and Dynamic Business Rules*). Dynamic business rules are rules that only apply at a certain point in time, namely when a query event or a mutation event occurs. The behavior of objects is largely determined by such dynamic business rules.

Examples of dynamic business rules are:

- A plane cannot be assigned a flight during the time it is in maintenance.
- A plane cannot be withdrawn as long as it is still scheduled for flights.

If we take a closer look at these business rules, we recognize that they refer to certain events on the one hand, and to states of the object on the other hand:

- The mutation event **assigning a flight to a plane** is not permitted in the state in maintenance of the object plane.
- The mutation event **withdrawing plane** is not permitted in the state **flights scheduled** of the object plane.
- The mutation event **starting plane** is not permitted in the state in transit of the object plane.

In other words: For certain events it should be possible to determine if an event is permitted in the current state of the object, and how the object will react to the event.

Consider the dynamic business rules that could apply to the object plane ticket in a passenger services system.

In the behavioral view, one statechart diagram per class is used to document which dynamic business rules have to be followed, and which events are allowed in which states of objects. In the simplest case, all events are allowed. Figure 4.44 shows a simple statechart diagram for the class frequent flyer card:

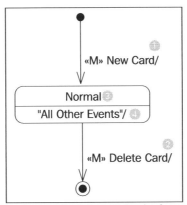

Figure 4.44 Simple statechart diagram for the frequent flyer card

A new object is created by the event «**M**» **New Card** (1). An object is deleted by the event «**M**» **Delete Card** (2). In between the object is in the state **Normal** (3), in which **"all other events"** (4) are allowed (in a real statechart diagram the events that are actually allowed have to be listed by name instead of the event "all other events").

If, however, we add business rules, the statechart diagram becomes more complex. We would like to amend our statechart diagram with the following rules:

- It has to be possible to suspend and reinstate a frequent flyer card.

- It is not possible to add any miles to a suspended frequent flyer card.

If we amend our statechart diagram with the mentioned dynamic business rules, the diagram depicted in Figure 4.45 is created:

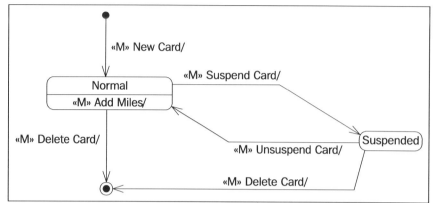

Figure 4.45 More complex statechart diagram for the frequent flyer card

A statechart diagram, such as the one of the frequent flyer card in Figure 4.45, shows on which paths or within which boundaries the life of a frequent flyer card object can proceed. In the diagram, possible and impossible chains of events can be recognized. A possible flow is, for instance, «M» **new card**, «M» **add miles**, «M> **add miles**, «M» **add miles**, «M» **suspend card**, «M» **delete card**.

An example of a sequence that is not permitted is: «M» **new card**, «M» **add miles**, «M» **add miles**, «M» **suspend card**, «M» **add miles**, «M» **delete card**. The second to last event, «M» **add miles**, is not accepted. If the card were unsuspended, miles could be added to it again.

Consider whether or not the following chains of events are permitted according to the statechart diagram of the class frequent flyer card in Figure 4.45:

- «M» **add miles**, «M» **add miles**, «M» **add miles**, «M» **delete card**, «M» **delete card**.

- «M» **new card**, «M» **add miles**, «M» **suspend card**, «M» **unsuspend card**, «M» **add miles**, «M» **delete card**.

- «M» **new card**, «M» **add miles**, «M» **suspend card**, «M» **suspend card**, «M» **delete card**.

Generally, the life of an object follows such a predetermined course, meaning that the object has to follow certain rules. Thus, the behavioral view is especially important, because it is the job of the IT system to ensure that these rules are followed. It is important that rules are documented in a correct and complete manner, to avoid misunderstandings on both the user side and the developer side. In a completed IT system, it should not be possible for a user to delete or modify objects when it is not permitted by business rules.

In the Hanseatic Merchant's trading office, an object corresponds to a book, for instance, the order book, and the clerk who is responsible for that book. The statechart diagram of the object contains the rules that the clerk has to follow when he handles the book. It is his instruction manual. It states, for example, that an order that has already been delivered, but that is not yet paid for, cannot be canceled. If you could sit next to the clerk for a while and watch him do his work, you would be able to see everything that can happen with an order in the order book. It can, for example, be recorded, modified, delivered, canceled, or paid for. The statechart diagram of the behavioral view contains the result of this object observation.

4.3.2. The Elements of the View

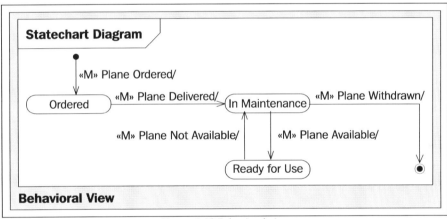

Figure 4.46 Behavioral view

The behavioral view, illustrated in Figure 4.46, consists of many statechart diagrams, each of which shows the behavior of an individual object. Therefore, all the statechart diagrams combined show the behavior of all the objects of the IT system. However, in practice, most often not all statechart diagrams are constructed but only those that:

- Contain many or important business rules or
- Describe important objects

4.3.3 Statechart Diagram

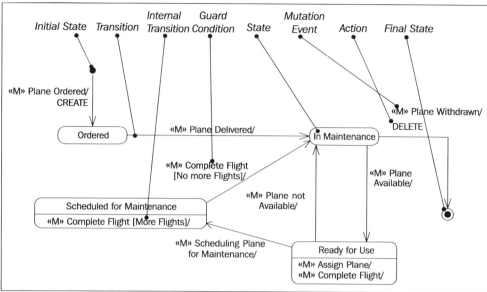

Figure 4.47 Elements of the statechart diagram

In statechart diagrams, as shown in Figure 4.47, we work with the following elements:

Initial State

The initial state represents the source of all objects:

It is not a normal state, because objects in this state do not yet exist.

State

The state of an object is always determined by its attributes and associations. States in statechart diagrams represent a **set** of those value combinations, in which an object **behaves the same** in response to events:

Therefore, not every modification of an attribute leads to a new state.

Transition

A transition represents the change from one state to another:

Internal Transition

An internal transition is a transition from one state to itself. This means that the object handles the event without changing its state:

The events that initiate the internal transition are listed in the lower part of the state symbol. For instance, a frequent flyer card object in the state normal remains in the state normal when the event «**M**» **add miles** occurs.

Mutation Event

A mutation event is the initiator of a transition from one state to another, or for an internal transition, where the state remains the same:

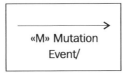

Action

An action is the activity of an object that is initiated by an event:

An action describes what the object does in response to the event. This description can be textual or formalized.

Guard Condition

A guard condition is a condition that has to be met in order to enable the transition to which it belongs:

Guard conditions can be used to document that a certain event, depending on the condition, can lead to different transitions.

Final State

The final state represents the end of an object's existence:

A final state is not a real state, because objects in this state do not exist anymore.

Reading Statechart Diagrams

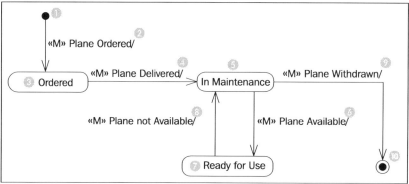

Figure 4.48 A Statechart diagram with events

The diagram in Figure 4.48 shows all states that the object plane can be in during the course of its life. Furthermore, it shows the possible transitions between the states and the events that initiate these transitions.

Each object of the class plane comes from nowhere (1) (initial state) and disappears (generally) again, into nothing (10) (final state). This usually holds true for all classes, meaning in most classes you will find an initial state (1) and a final state (10).

Over the course of its life, an plane (please note: we are here talking about the object plane and not about a real airplane) can take up three states: **ordered** (3), **in maintenance** (5), and **ready for use** (7)

The event **«M» plane ordered**, leads to the occurrence, that from nowhere (1) a new plane object is created in the IT system (birth). Immediately after it has been created it is in the state **ordered** (3).

If the event **«M» plane delivered** (4) occurs, and the plane is the state **ordered** (3), it changes to the state **in maintenance** (5). If the plane is in any other state than ordered, nothing happens.

Through the events **«M» plane available** (6) and **«M»plane not available** (8), the plane changes any number of times between the states **in maintenance** (5) and **ready for use** (7).

At the end of its life, the airplane object disappears through the event **«M»plane withdrawn** (9) into nothing (10), meaning it will be deleted (death).

Figure 4.49 shows more elements that can occur in statechart diagrams:

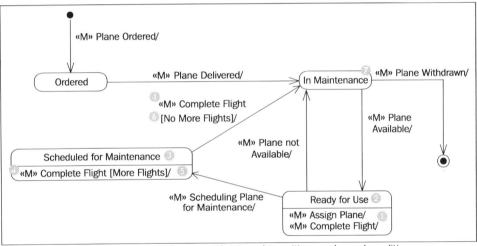

Figure 4.49 Statechart diagram with internal transitions and guard conditions.

In addition to the transitions we have already explained, there are also internal transitions. The event **«M» assign plane** (1), which occurs when the plane is assigned to a flight, initiates no transition to another state. Rather, the plane remains in the state **ready for use** (2). This constitutes an internal transition; the plane object is in the same state **ready for use** (2) before and after the event.

A guard condition allows acceptance or rejection of an event depending on a condition. If in the state **scheduled for maintenance** (3) the event **«M» complete flight** (4) occurs, the response of the object depends on the guard condition stated in brackets. If the condition [**more flights**] (5) is true (meaning there are more flights assigned to the plane) an internal transition takes place. The plane remains in the state **scheduled for maintenance** (3). However, if the condition [**no more flights**] is true (meaning no other flights are assigned to the plane) a transition to the state **in maintenance** (7) takes place.

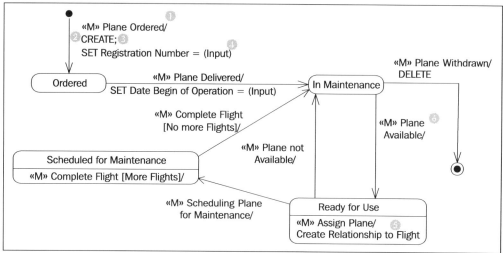

Figure 4.50 Statechart diagram

Actions indicate how an object responds to a mutation event. Figure 4.50 shows several types of actions. An action always follows the slash (1) after the event. The actions **CREATE** (2) and **SET registration number** = (**input**) (4) follow the mutation event «**M**» **plane ordered**. **CREATE** indicates that a new object is created; **SET registration number** = (**input**) indicates that a value, which the user entered in the use case, is assigned to the attribute registration number. Individual actions are divided by a semicolon (;) (3). In addition to these semi-formal actions, such as CREATE and SET (see Section 4.3.4, Constructing Statechart Diagrams), actions can also be described in free text. Following the mutation event «**M**» **assign plane** is the action **create relationship to flight** (5), which indicates that a relationship to a flight object is created. If no action is stated for an event (6), this can either mean that the action has not yet been specified, or that the object merely transitions into another state.

Gaining a deeper understanding of our case study, you will notice that the statechart diagram in Figure 4.50 will have to be amended with further states and events.

A statechart diagram that documents all possible paths of an object cannot simply be read in a sequential manner. However, it helps the reader to answer several typical questions:

- What happens to the object if a certain event occurs? Since the answer to this question in each case depends on the current state of the object, the question should really be:

- How does an object in a certain state respond to a certain event?

- Which events are relevant for the object?

- How, meaning through which events, can a certain state be left?

- How, meaning though which events, can a certain state be achieved?

Let's try to answer some of these questions by looking at the statechart diagram of the class plane in Figure 4.51:

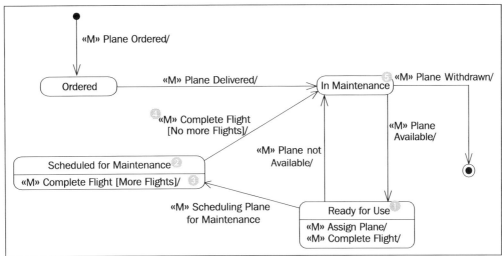

Figure 4.51 Selective reading of a statechart diagram

- How does a **plane** object in the state **ready for use** (1) react to the event «**M**» **assign plane**? In order to answer this question, we have to check first if the event «**M**» **assign plane** even exists in the state **ready for use** (1). The event is allowed if a transition (an arrow) to another state exists that is labeled with the event name, or if an internal transition exists (an entry in the lower part of the state symbol). In our example, a transition to another state does not exist but an internal transition does. This means: A **plane** object in the state **ready for use** (1) accepts the event «**M**» **assign plane** and remains in the state **ready for use** (1).

- How does a **plane** object in the state **scheduled for maintenance** (2) react to the event «**M**» **complete flight**? In order to answer this question we check first if the event «**M**» **complete flight** even exists in the state **scheduled for maintenance** (2). In our example, we have a transition to another state, as well as an internal transition. Since only one transition is possible, (the plane object is supposed to be in exactly one definite state and not two) we need criteria in order to determine which transition is supposed to take place. Here, we have the help of the guard conditions [**more flights**] (3) and [**no**

more flights] (4). We have to check if there are more flights assigned to the plane. In our case we assume that no more flights are assigned to the plane. This means: A **plane** object in the state **scheduled for maintenance** (2) accepts the event «**M**» **complete flight** and transitions to the state **in maintenance** (5), since no more flights are assigned to it.

- How does a **plane** object in the state **scheduled for maintenance** (2) react to the event «**M**» **assign flight**? In order to answer this question, we check first if the event «**M**» **assign flight** even exists in the state **scheduled for maintenance** (2). In our example, neither a transition to another state nor an internal transition exists. This means: A **plane** object in the state **scheduled for maintenance** (2) does not accept the event «**M**» **assign plane**. (The IT system should inform the user about the reason why assigning the plane did not work.)

- Which events are relevant for a **plane** object? The answer is: All events that are contained in the statechart diagram of the class **plane**, meaning all events that are accepted in at least one state. All other events are not relevant for the plane object. This means: The only events relevant for a plane object are «**M**» **plane ordered**, «**M**» **plane delivered**, «**M**» **plane available**, «**M**» **plane not available**, «**M**» **assign plane**, «**M**» **complete flight**, «**M**» **scheduling plane for maintenance**, and «**M**» **plane withdrawn**.

- Through which event can the plane object leave the state **in maintenance** (5)? In order to answer this question, we search all transitions (arrows) that go from the state **in maintenance** (5) to another state. Our example has two such transitions. This means: A plane object in the state in maintenance (5) can only leave this state through the event «**M**» **plane available**, or «**M**» **plane withdrawn**.

- Through which events does a plane object reach the state ready for use (1)? In order to answer this question, we search for all transitions (arrows) that lead to the state **ready for use** (1). Our example has exactly one such transition. This means: A plane object can only reach the state **ready for use** (1) though the event «**M**» **plane available** (namely, from the state in maintenance (2)).

The questions discussed have already shown that in statechart diagrams, what is not written is just as important as what is written. Events that do not exist in a certain state are not accepted if the object is in this state. This means that an event that was not accepted cannot be successfully executed within the IT system. An appropriate error message has to be generated. Events that do not exist in any state are always ignored. The following statements can be read from the statechart diagram for the plane object:

- If a plane is delivered it is never directly in the state ready for use, it is always first in the state in maintenance.

- A plane ready for use cannot be withdrawn. If this is attempted anyway, the mutation event fails with an appropriate error message.

4.3.4 Constructing Statechart Diagrams

The following checklist shows the necessary steps for constructing the statechart diagrams of a class. Subsequently, we will explain the individual steps further.

Checklist 4.6 Constructing Statechart Diagrams in the Behavioral View:

- Identify mutation events relevant for the object—What affects the object?

- Group relevant events chronologically—How does a normal life look?

- Model states and transitions—Which states are there?

- Add actions to the statechart diagram—What do objects do?

- Verify the statechart diagram—Is everything correct?

Identify Mutation Events Relevant for the Object—What Affects the Object?

First, we have to find out which mutation events are relevant for an object, meaning, which mutation events initiate actions, a state transition, or both for an object. The following questions will help you find relevant mutation events for objects:

- Which mutation events lead to the creation or deletion of an object?

- Which mutation events define or modify attribute values?

- Which mutation events create relationships to other objects or end these relationships?

- Which mutation events result in a state transition of the object?

- Which mutation events from the use case sequence diagram of the external view affect the object?

The answers to these questions lead to a list of mutation events that are relevant for the object. Since all mutation events originate from use cases, a new use case has to be found for each new mutation event that is not already contained in the use case sequence diagram. An event that is not sent to the IT system within the scope of a use case is never sent to the IT system. This can lead to the fact that new use cases have to be modeled.

In the case study, we found the following relevant mutation events for the object flight:

«M» **flight defined**, «M» **flight started**, «M» **flight landed**, «M» **flight canceled**, «M» **new flight date**, «M» **flight irrelevant**, and «M» **flight number irrelevant**.

Group Relevant Events Chronologically—How Does a Normal Life Look?

The obtained mutation events are divided into three groups: events that lead to the creation of new objects (birth), events that are important during the existence of an object (life), and events that lead to the deletion of an object (death). The question is:

- To which stage of the life of an object does each mutation event belong?

The mutation events from our case study for the object flight can be grouped as follows:

- Birth: «M» **flight defined**
- Life: «M» **flight started**, «M» **flight landed**, «M» **flight canceled**, and «M» **new flight date**
- Death: «M» **flight irrelevant** and «M» **flight number irrelevant**

Model States and Transitions—Which States are There?

As a first draft, you can always construct a very simple statechart diagram, consisting of the initial state, a normal state, and the final state. Figure 4.52 shows such a diagram for the object flight:

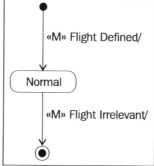

Figure 4.52 Simple statechart diagram

Starting with this simple diagram, the obtained mutation events can be added. Here, the following questions should be asked for each event:

- Is the mutation event permitted in all cases, meaning, for all states, or are there states in which the mutation event is not permitted? The various cases that decide if a mutation event is permitted are depicted as states. Behind these cases are the dynamic business rules, which we already mentioned in Section 4.2.3, *Static and Dynamic Business Rules*.

- In which state is the object after the occurrence of a mutation event?
  The new state depends on the state of the object before the occurrence of the mutation event.

- Does the transition to a new state depend on certain conditions? We can use guard conditions to document that a mutation event—depending on a condition—can lead to different new states (see Figure 4.49).

For instance, in our case study, the event «**M**» **flight started** is permitted only if the flight is not already in the state in transit. When all questions have been answered for all mutation events, a statechart diagram such as the one in Figure 4.53 has been created:

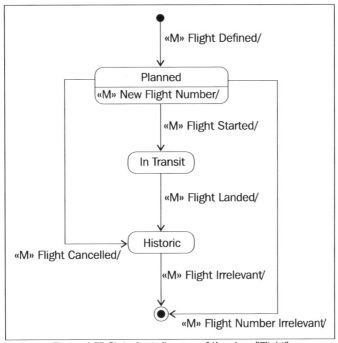

Figure 4.53 Statechart diagram of the class "Flight"

Add Actions to the Statechart Diagram—What do Objects Do?

After the mutation events of an object have been found and modeled, their consequences are specified in form of actions. The following questions have to be answered:

- Where are actions needed for dealing with attribute values?
- Where are actions needed for dealing with relationships?
- Where else are actions needed (activating queries, calculations)?

The required actions are inserted into the statechart diagram. In the level of detail that we are using for statechart diagrams, it is not a problem to describe actions informally, in plain English. However, our practical experience has shown that a certain level of formality works better, where keywords are used for frequent actions:

- **CREATE/DELETE**: Creates or deletes an object of a class (can also be omitted, since it is implied).

- **SET** <attribute> := ...: Sets the value of an attribute.

- **TIE TO** <object>/CUT FROM <object>: Establishes relationship to another object or breaks the relationship to another object.

Figure 4.54 shows the statechart diagram for the class flight from the case study with actions:

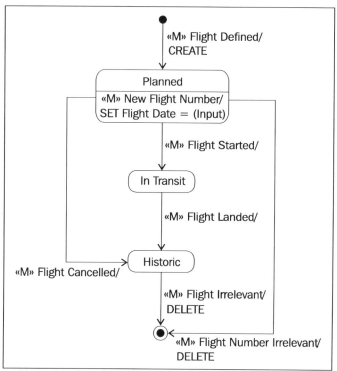

Figure 4.54 Statechart diagram of the class "Flight" with actions

Verify Statechart Diagram—Is Everything Correct?

The completed statechart diagram can be verified with the following checklist:

Checklist 4.7 Verifying Statechart Diagrams of the Behavioral View:

- Is there a formulated final state, or does the object live eternally without a death event?

- Is there an (indirect) transition from every state to the final state?

- Is there a differentiation, if it is relevant, between logical death (freezing of the object) and physical death (deletion of the object)?

- Does at least one specific event exist for each state, to which a specific response occurs only from this state? If not, this state should be corrected.

- If two or more transitions that are initiated by the same event leave the same state, the guard conditions must be **disjunct** (meaning they can't be true at the same time).

4.4 Interaction View

4.4.1 Seeing What Happens Inside the IT System

In most cases, the mere highlighting of structures is not sufficient for understanding a system. Even with a detailed plan of an oil refinery, it is difficult to understand how oil is converted into gasoline. Only when the process (flow) of refining is explained does it become understandable. Identifying flows is a powerful tool for explaining something. This is also true for models of the IT system. The static view of classes alone is not enough to understand an IT system. For instance, what happens in the IT system when a passenger checks in? Which flows are being processed? Which objects are affected? These questions are answered by the interaction view.

Just as important is the fact that modeling the interaction view contributes much to the verification and completion of the static view. By having to deal with class diagrams from modeling queries to the level of individual attributes, it is ensured that the class diagram meets all requirements. Which aspect is important depends on how complete the class diagram is at the point of modeling the interaction view.

- A fairly complete class diagram is verified by modeling the interaction view.
- An incomplete class diagram is enhanced and completed by modeling the interaction view.

A close relationship exists between the interaction view and use cases. Use cases show the external view. The IT system is viewed as a black box. In the interaction view, this black box is opened and what occurs inside the IT system is revealed. The interaction view illustrates which objects are needed for the processing of a certain task and how objects communicate with each other. UML uses two diagram types to model the interaction view: the communication diagram and the sequence diagram. In the course of this section, we will explain these diagrams further:

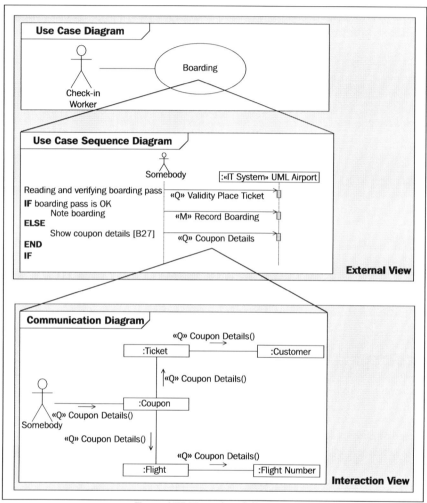

Figure 4.55 Hierarchy of diagrams

Figure 4.55 shows the relationship between use cases and a communication diagram of the interaction view:

- At the top you can see a use case diagram with the use case **boarding**.

- The use case **boarding** is described in a use case sequence diagram. Essentially, this description consists of a chain of query events and mutation events.

- The flow of each **query event** is described in a communication diagram.

With mutation events the process is analogous: their flow has been described in sequence diagrams.

In order to correctly understand diagrams of the interaction view, we would like to show here how an object-oriented system works on the inside. A system functions through objects, which either perform work themselves or delegate work to other objects. This is exactly how the IT system is modeled with UML. Here, it is not important whether or not the IT system is implemented with object-oriented technology. The IT system is modeled at a high level of abstraction, which is disconnected from design and programming:

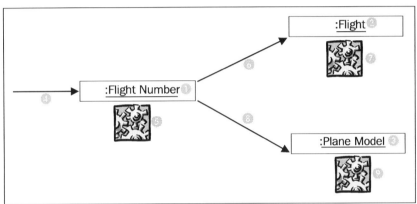

Figure 4.56 Cooperation of objects

Figure 4.56 shows the cooperation of three objects in an IT system: **a flight number** object (1), a **flight object** (2), and **a plane model** object (3). The task is to delete a flight number (e.g. SR9011) in the IT system.

In our model, from the use case **canceling flight number** a **mutation event** (4) is sent to the **flight number** object (1). Now the **flight number** object can become active (5), for instance, it can verify if the deletion is possible. It can also forward (6) (8) the event to other objects (2) (3) that need to become active (7) (9).

Exactly this kind of cooperation between objects is documented in communication diagrams and sequence diagrams of the interaction view. Here, the focus is on involved objects and sent events. What occurs within the objects, meaning the behavior of individual objects (the modification of attribute values, calculations, deletion of objects, etc.), cannot be seen in these diagrams. The behavior of objects is defined in the behavioral view. The behavioral view shows for each object what exactly happens when a certain event reaches that object.

In the Hanseatic Merchant's trading office, the interaction view would be documented as follows: You go to secretary Hildebrand and watch him perform a task, for example, cashing a bond. Here, you record in which order he goes to the individual clerks with their books, in order to ask them something (query) or to order them to change something in the book (mutation).

The cooperation of objects shown in Figure 4.56 is based on the mechanism of sending events, meaning that objects can send each other events and therefore, initiate certain events. However, in order to send an event to a particular object, the object has to be known. If, for example, an event is supposed to be sent from a ticket object to the corresponding customer object, this is only possible if the ticket object knows what its customer object is. Exactly this information is documented in the class diagrams of the static view:

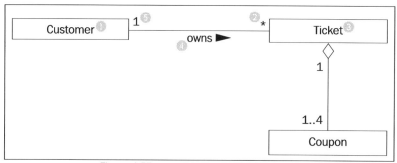

Figure 4.57 Associations in a class diagram

The excerpt from the class diagram shown in Figure 4.57 states that a **customer** (1) owns (4) zero, one, or several (2) **tickets** (3), and that a **ticket** is owned by exactly one (5) **customer** (see Section 4.2.5, *Class Diagram*). For the objects that are generated from the classes of this diagram this means:

- Each **customer** object "knows" the **ticket** objects that are assigned to it.
- Each **ticket** object "knows" the **coupon** objects that are assigned to it.

Objects that are connected to each other know each other. This is the prerequisite for it to be possible for events to be sent. Normally in the interaction view events are sent along associations in class diagrams. An alternative is to attach the identification of an object to which an event is supposed to be sent as an event parameter.

The UML diagrams that we use to illustrate the interaction view, sequence diagrams, and communication diagrams, are combined under the generic term interaction diagrams. Both diagrams allow for a similar view of the IT system. Both diagrams show the flow of cooperation between objects, namely their interactions. However, the two diagrams differ in the following points:

- In sequence diagrams, a chronological sequence becomes immediately apparent. A vertical time axis indicates a clear sequence from top to bottom. Communication diagrams do not have this time axis. Possible sequences have to be documented by numbering events.

- Communication diagrams are more similar to the static class diagram. Class names and attributes can be shown. This makes it possible that certain flows, such as reading of information, can be documented in a simple manner. In sequence diagrams, we cannot illustrate which attributes are to be read from an object.

- Communication diagrams work well to show parallel paths of interactions. Although this is also possible with sequence diagrams, sequence diagrams easily become too complex.

These differences are the reasons behind our selection of diagram types. Communication diagrams are especially suited to the documentation of query events, in which attributes are read and where objects do not perform any further work. Sequence diagrams are better suited to the documentation of mutation events, in which objects perform substantial work, and in which sequence is rather important.

4.4.2 Elements of the View

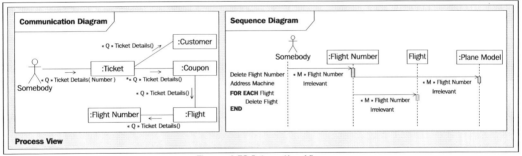

Figure 4.58 Interaction View

The interaction view of IT systems, illustrated in Figure 4.58, consists of two elements:

- **Communication diagrams** document the flow of **queries** within the IT system. Each query is part of a use case.

- **Sequence diagrams** document the flow of **mutation events** within the IT system. Mutation events are also part of a use case.

Both diagrams show how objects of the IT system cooperate in the processing of events. In this way, each query event from the use cases becomes its own communication diagram, and each mutation event becomes its own sequence diagram.

In reality, we do not document every flow of every query and every mutation. The effort for this would be too much. We only document those flows that are especially important or complex. The following considerations should help making the right choices:

- For each query event we have to verify if all necessary classes, attributes, and associations are present in the class diagram. For simple queries it can be sufficient to check off the necessary data elements on a printout (see Section 4.4.5, *Constructing Communication Diagrams*). For such queries a communication diagram is not needed. This work step further helps to verify or complete class diagrams.

- Queries that are very important to the user, or that are very complex, should be documented in a communication diagram.

4.4.3 Communication Diagram

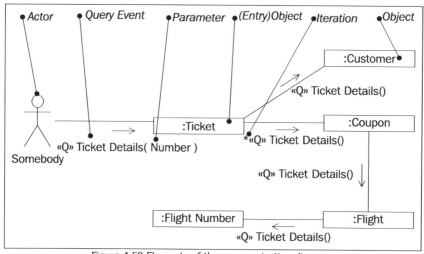

Figure 4.59 Elements of the communication diagram

In communication diagrams, as illustrated in Figure 4.59, we work with the following elements:

Actor "Somebody"

Actor **"somebody"** represents any actor from a use case diagram. Since the query event that is documented in the communication diagram can be contained in several use cases, and since these use cases have different actors, we use the actor "somebody":

In this way, we do not have to commit ourselves to a particular actor. (In communication diagrams actors can also be omitted altogether. In our experience, however, this makes the diagrams hard to understand.)

Query Event

A query event represents a query for information:

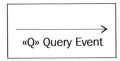

Normally, a query event from a use case is sent to the IT system, for example, a query for detailed information about a ticket.

Parameter

Parameters allow for attaching information to an event, e.g., the number of a ticket, so that the correct ticket can be read:

Iteration

An iteration indicates that all objects to which an association exists receive the event, for instance, all the coupons of a ticket:

Object and Entry Object

The object represents an object of a class in the static view, for instance, "Henry Johnson", who is an object of the class **passenger**:

Object:Class

The entry object is the first object that receives a query event from an actor. At the entry object the interaction path begins.

Reading Communication Diagrams

Figure 4.60 shows a communication diagram with the actor **somebody** and the objects **ticket**, **customer**, **coupon**, **flight**, and **flight number**. The diagram documents the flow of the query «**Q**» **coupon details**.

Starting on the left, the communication diagram is read as follows: Actor **somebody** (1) sends the query event, «**Q**» **coupon details** (2) to an object of the class **coupon** (3).

Actor "Somebody"

In our IT system model, use cases are the source of events. What is documented in this communication diagram occurs in the context of a use case. It has proven to be of value to use the undefined actor **somebody** (1) instead of the actor of the use case. The flow of an event that is described in the communication diagram can occur in various use cases with different actors. The actor **somebody** (1) substitutes for the actor of the use case from which the query event «**Q**» **coupon details** (2) stems:

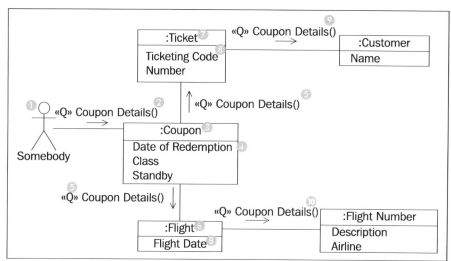

Figure 4.60 Communication diagram

The **coupon object** (3) provides its attributes—**date of redemption**, **class**, and **standby** (4)—and forwards the query event «**Q**» **coupon details** (5) to two other objects: to the **flight** object (6) that belongs to the coupon, and to the **ticket** object (7) that belongs to the **coupon**.

These two objects, in turn, provide certain attributes (8) and then forward the query event «**Q**» **coupon details** (9, 10). In this way, the communication diagram can be used to document the "collection" of attributes as a reaction to a query event.

Unlike sequence diagrams, communication diagrams do not have time dimensions. Objects can be spread across the diagrams in any way. An order in which events are processed can only be partially seen from them:

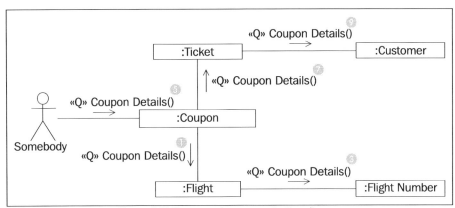

Figure 4.61 Sequence in communication diagram

The following statements can be made about the sequence in the diagram in Figure 4.61 (the numbers in the descriptions were intentionally assigned to avoid implying any particular order):

- First, the event is sent from the actor **somebody** to the **coupon** (5).
- After that a sequence is not defined:
    - On the one hand, the event goes to the **flight** (1) and subsequently to the **flight number** (3).
    - On the other hand, the event goes to the **ticket** (7) and subsequently to the **customer** (9).

The event flow branches at the coupon, without noting an order. In most cases, order is unimportant anyway. However, should order be important, UML allows numbering the sequence of events in a communication diagram.

Iteration indicates that all reachable objects and not just one particular object are addressed:

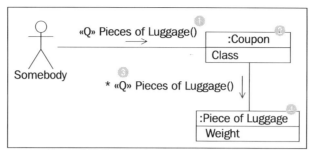

Figure 4.62 Iteration in communication diagram

We can read in Figure 4.62 that the query event «**Q**» **pieces of luggage** (1) is first sent to a **coupon** object (2) and from there is sent to **all** (3) (iteration) connected **pieces of luggage** (4). The iteration is documented with an asterisk (*) in front of the event name.

4.4.4 Sequence Diagram

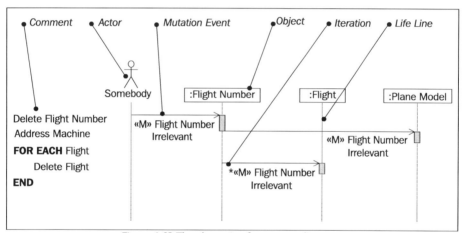

Figure 4.63 The elements of sequence diagrams

In sequence diagrams, as shown in Figure 4.63, we work with the following elements:

Comment

The flow of a mutation event is documented with a combination of textual description and a sequence diagram:

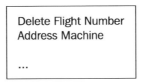

In comments, the flow logic is shown on the topmost level.

Actor "Somebody"

The actor "somebody" represents any actor from the use case diagram. Since the mutation event that is documented in a sequence diagram can be contained in several use cases, and since these use cases can have different actors, we use the actor somebody:

This way, we do not have to decide on one, specific, actor.

Mutation Event

A mutation event is an event that is sent from the use case, so normally from the user interface, to the IT system:

The goal of the event is to mutate information in the IT system, meaning to create, change, or delete something.

Object

An object represents any object, meaning an undefined object of a class of the IT system:

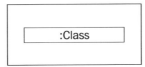

Iteration

An iteration indicates that all objects to which a relationship exists receive the event, for example all the flights of a flight number:

Lifeline

The lifeline of an object represents a life (over the course of time). The rectangle, meaning the "thick part" of the lifeline shows when the object is active:

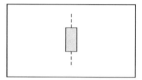

(The aspect of activation is not important for our use of sequence diagrams.)

Reading Sequence Diagrams

Figure 4.64 shows a sequence diagram with objects of the classes **flight number**, **flight**, and **plane model**. The diagram, as a whole, documents the flow of the mutation «**M**» **flight number irrelevant**:

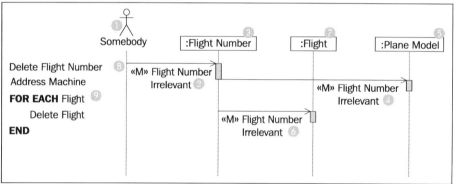

Figure 4.64 A sequence diagram

The diagram can be read from top to bottom. The flow starts with the **actor** (1) sending the mutation event «**M**» **flight number irrelevant** (2) to an object of the **class flight number** (3).

The background to this (just like the communication diagrams), is that the use case is the source of the mutation event. In the sequence diagram, the **actor** (1) represents the use case.

How the event is processed within the flight number object cannot be seen in the sequence diagram. Clues can only be found in the comment (8). An exact description of the processing can be found in the statechart diagram (see Section 4.3, *The Behavioral View*) of the class flight number.

Further, it can be read in the diagram that the object of **class flight number** (3) forwards the mutation event «**M**» **flight number irrelevant** (4) to an object of the class **plane model** (5). Again, the processing of the event within the object remains invisible. The processing of the events is completed in the **plane model** object (5), and the control goes back to the sender of the event, so to the **flight number** object (3). No separate event arrow is inserted for the "reply", after processing is completed.

Finally, the mutation event «**Q**» **flight number irrelevant** (6) is sent to the object of class **flight** (7). Since it is possible that a flight number objects knows many **flight** objects (this information can be taken from the class diagram of the static view), the mutation event is sent to all **flight** objects of the **flight number** object. The iteration asterisk * at the event (1) in the sequence diagram (Figure 4.65) marks this process. However, we recommend annotating the diagram with an additional comment in the left margin (2), in order to make the diagram easier to read:

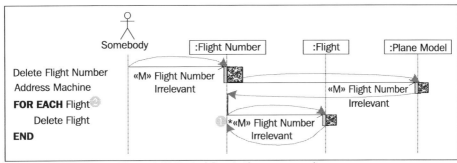

Figure 4.65 Control flow in the sequence diagram

Figure 4.65 shows the control flow in a sequence diagram. We use the sequence diagram only to document mutation events. UML provides many more possibilities for the use of this diagram type. However, our practical experience has shown that less is often more, and that we can sufficiently communicate the essential aspects of the interaction view with this restricted use of sequence diagrams.

4.4.5 Constructing Communication Diagrams

The following checklist shows the necessary steps for constructing a communication diagram per query event from the use cases. Subsequently, we will explain the individual steps further.

Checklist 4.8 Constructing Communication Diagrams in the Interaction View:

- Draft query result—What do we want?

- Identify involved classes—Which classes do we need?

- Define initial object—Where do we start?

- Design event path—Where do we go?

- Amend event path—Exactly which objects do we need?

- Identify necessary attributes—What exactly do we want to know?

- Verify the communication diagram—Is everything correct?

Draft Query Result—What do We Want?

The starting point for modeling a query event is the expected result. Generally, the desired result is a display on the monitor or a printed document, for instance, a list or a receipt. Figure 4.66 shows a window from the prototype of an IT system, and Figure 4.67 a section of a boarding pass.

For each query event to be documented in a communication diagram we need to know what the result is supposed to look like. The following questions have to be asked:

- How (exactly) is the result of a query supposed to look?

- Which elements should the results contain; which of them are fixed texts and which of them are data elements?

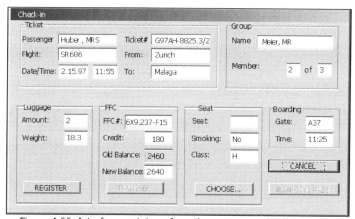

Figure 4.66: Interface prototype from the passenger check-in system

We recommend that you sketch the result. For each element of the sketch you should indicate whether we are dealing with information from the IT system or a fixed element, for example, a picture or field labels. In a screen form, field labels normally do not come from information in the IT system. However, if the IT system supports several languages, it is possible that the field labels are taken from information in the IT system. Another example is the boarding pass, for which a pre-printed form is used, meaning that the field labels already exist. The pass merely has to be completed with information read form the IT system. In Figure 4.67, the fields of the boarding pass that receive information from the IT system are circled.

The boarding pass from our case study contains the following data elements:

ECONOMY, GRAESSLE, PATRIC, MR,ZURICH, HERAKLION, EDW761, Y, 29MAY0745, B38, 0715, NO, 2, and 34.

The goal of the modeling of the communication diagram is to show how the values listed can be derived from the class diagram.

Figure 4.67 Part of a boarding pass

Identify Involved Classes—Which Classes Do We Need?

From the sketched result, we can determine the necessary classes from the class diagram.

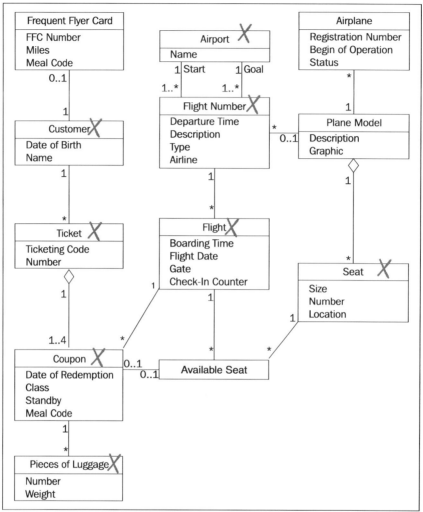

Figure 4.68 Marked (simplified) class diagram

The questions are:

- From which classes is information supposed to be read? We need to determine from which attributes and classes each information element in the sketched result is calculated.

- Which classes are needed for the access path? Classes are either needed on the basis of their attributes, which are necessary to generate query results, or on the basis of their relationships to other classes.

- Which classes are missing in the class diagram? Depending on the level of completion of the class diagram, it could happen that new, additional classes have to be modeled.

In a first draft, the needed classes can simply be marked by hand on a printout of the class diagram. In Figure 4.68, the classes needed to generate the boarding pass from Figure 4.67 are marked.

Define Initial Object—Where Do We Start?

The query begins with the initial object. The initial object can be a class (in its function as a set) or a particular object of a class. If a certain object is addressed directly, for instance, a certain customer object, or a certain ticket object, this object has to be known before the query event is sent. If a class is addressed, parameters can be attached to the query as selection parameters, so that a particular object can be chosen. All further needed classes have to be accessible from the initial object through connections. The concrete questions are:

- Which is the first object the event is supposed to go to?

- Which object do I know already?

- Where do I start collecting information?

To generate a boarding pass in our case study, we begin with the coupon of the plane ticket for which we want to generate the boarding pass.

Design Event Path—Where Do We Go?

Starting from the initial object, we determine a path through which the needed objects can be reached. The question is:

- Through which path can I reach all needed objects in the class diagram?

For a first draft, this path can, in turn, be marked by hand on the printout of the class diagram. Figure 4.69 shows the completely marked class diagram for the query event generating a boarding pass:

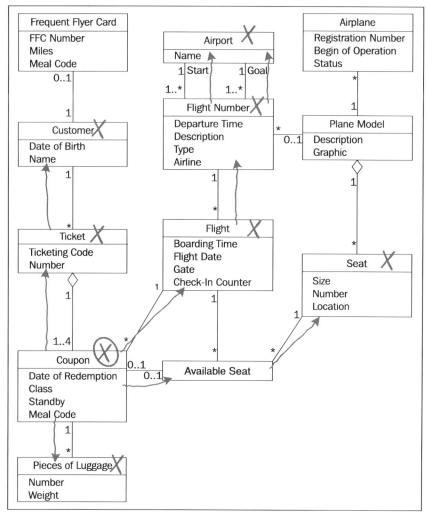

Figure 4.69 (Simplified) Class diagram with event path

In many cases, it is sufficient to mark the event path by hand in the class diagram. With that, you have documented that the query, in our case generating a boarding pass, is possible with the class diagram. In this case, it can be done without modeling a communication diagram. However, for complex or important queries, we recommend that you generate a communication diagram for the query, on the basis of this marked class diagram. All marked classes are transferred to this, and the query event is inserted along the event path. Figure 4.70 shows the result of this work step:

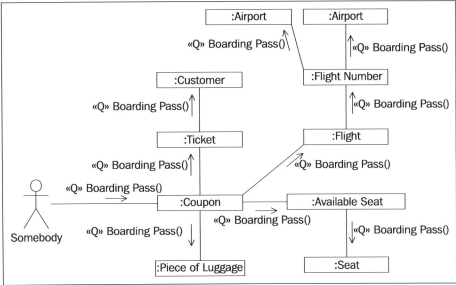

Figure 4.70 First draft of the communication diagram

Amend Event Path—Exactly Which Objects do We Need?

The event path has to be filled out with selections and iterations. Selections and iterations are used if along a path several objects of one class can be reached from another class, meaning, when the multiplicity of an association in the class diagram has an upper limit larger than 1 (usually *). In such cases we need to state whether all objects should be iterated, or individual objects should be selected on the basis of certain criteria. The question is:

- If I encounter more than one object along my path, do I then need all of them (iteration), or do a need a particular one (selection)?

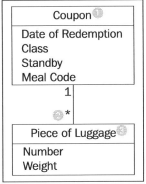

Figure 4.71 Selection or iteration?

In our case study, in Figure 4.71 we might encounter **several** (2) **pieces of luggage** (3) along the event path originating at **coupon** (1). We need all pieces of luggage for the boarding pass, because we want to print the number and total weight on the pass. Therefore, we have to iterate.

This is documented in the communication diagram in Figure 4.72 by the inconspicuous asterisk in from of the event name (4):

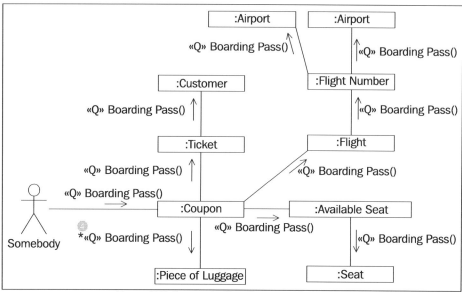

Figure 4.72 Communication diagram with iteration

Identify Necessary Attributes—What Exactly Do We Want to Know?

In the last step, we document the attributes that are needed to answer the query. The questions are:

- Which attributes are needed for the query result?

- Which attributes are missing in the class diagram?

Finally, all data elements from the drafted query result must be able to be traced back to the attributes in the class diagram of the static view. In the simplest case, this can be done, again, by marking attributes on a printout of the class diagram. When the communication diagram has been modeled, attributes can be inserted (Figure 4.73):

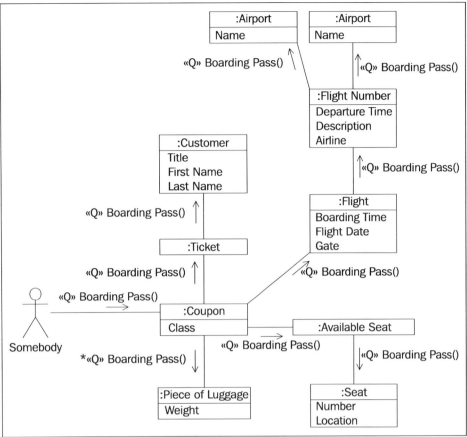

Figure 4.73 Communication diagram with attributes

Verify the Communication Diagram—Is Everything Correct?

The completed communication diagram can be verified with the following checklist:

Checklist 4.9 Verifying Communication Diagrams in the Interaction View:

- Can the drafted query result be constructed with the communication diagram?

- Do the event paths in the communication diagram flow along the associations in the class diagram?

- Does it always say where it is needed according to the class diagram, if we are dealing with an iteration or selection?

> • If the answer to all these questions is yes, most of the possible sources of mistakes have been eliminated.

4.4.6 Constructing Sequence Diagrams

The following checklist shows the necessary steps for constructing a sequence diagram per mutation event from the use cases. Subsequently, we will explain the individual steps further:

Checklist 4.10 Constructing Sequence Diagrams in the Interaction View:

• Identify involved classes—What is affected by mutation events?

• Determine initial object—Where does the mutation event go first?

• Propagate events—How is the mutation event forwarded?

• Specify event parameter—What do objects have to know?

• Verify the sequence diagram—Is everything correct?

Identify Involved Classes—What is Affected by Mutation Events?

The classes that a mutation event affects have to be identified. This occurs on the basis of statechart diagrams (see Section 4.3, *The Behavioral View*). The questions are:

• Which classes are already affected by a certain mutation event? To answer this question you will have to look up which statechart diagrams contain the mutation event. If the mutation event is present in a statechart diagram of a class, this class is affected by the mutation event, meaning that the mutation event has to be sent to this class.

• Which other classes are affected by the mutation diagram? It could be that there are classes that are affected by the mutation event, but which are not yet present in statechart diagrams.

The first question can easily be answered. Most CASE tools can generate, for instance, a list of classes already affected. In order to find further affected classes, look at the class diagram and think whether anything has to happen with the objects of each class when the mutation event occurs. At the least, you should take another look at those classes that are located close to some of the classes already affected on the class diagram. Of course, if additional classes are found, their statechart diagrams have to be updated by inserting the mutation event. In our case study, the mutation event «M» **record piece of luggage** affects the classes **coupon** and **piece of luggage**, as shown in Figure 4.74:

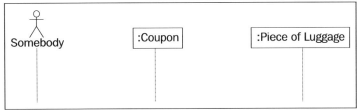

Figure 4.74 Affected classes in the sequence diagram

Determine Initial Object—Where does the Mutation Event go First?

A mutation starts with the initial object. The initial object can be a class (in its function as a set) or a particular object of a class. If a certain object is directly addressed, for example, a certain flight object or a certain ticket object, this object has to be known before the mutation event is sent. If a class is addressed, parameters can be attached to the mutation event as selection parameters, so that a particular object can be chosen. All further needed classes have to be accessible from the initial object through connections. The concrete questions are:

- Which is the first object the event should go to?
- Which object do I know already?
- Where do I start collecting information?

In our case study, during the mutation event «M» **record piece of luggage**, the **coupon** object is already known, since the entire check-in occurs for on a particular coupon. The new **piece of luggage** object that is to be recorded does not yet exist. Therefore, the initial object is the **coupon** object.

Propagate Events—How is the Mutation Event Forwarded?

Starting from the initial object, a sequence is determined, in which the affected objects receive the mutation event. The question is:

- In which order do I reach all affected objects in the class diagram?

Mutation events are forwarded along the relationships in the class diagram to all classes that are affected by the mutation event. In the class diagram of the case study an association exists from the coupon to a piece of luggage, along which a mutation event can be sent, as illustrated in Figure 4.75:

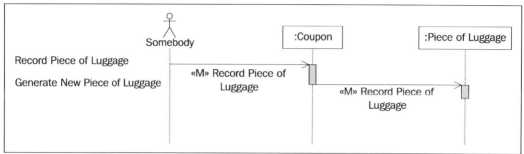

Figure 4.75 Events in a sequence diagram

Specify Event Parameter—What do Objects have to Know?

The information required to process the mutation event is forwarded as parameters of the event. The question is:

- Which information do the objects need in order to process the mutation?

In order to generate a new piece of luggage object in our case study, we need its weight. Therefore, weight will be forwarded as an event parameter, as shown in Figure 4.76:

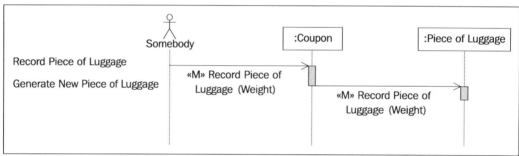

Figure 4.76 Event parameter in a sequence diagram

Verify the Sequence Diagram—Is Everything Correct?

The completed sequence diagram can be verified with the following checklist:

Checklist 4.11 Verifying Sequence Diagram in the Interaction View:

- Are all classes affected by the mutation event listed in the sequence diagram?

- Is the mutation event forwarded along an association in the class diagram?

If the answer to both these questions is yes, the largest sources of mistakes have been eliminated.

5

Modeling for System Integration

System Integration was long one of the least considered areas within information technology. Only recently, with the emergence of electronic business and Enterprise Application Integration (EAI), it is starting to receive more attention. Even though system integration has existed since the first two IT systems were connected by an interface, only in the last couple of years have standards for the fields of design, method, and implementation became established. This chapter illustrates how UML can be used to model messages and processes for the exchange of these messages.

We understand system integration to be the **embedding** of existing and new IT systems into an existing IT environment. Embedding can take place in-house, where we generate interfaces to other IT systems within the organization. Embedding can also span several organizations, where we connect the IT systems of different organizations. Whether the IT systems that need to be integrated in existing infrastructure and processes are within the organization (in-house) or external plays a minor role from a modeling perspective.

Integration of an IT system requires knowledge about the environment of the IT system and its borders. Since an IT system that needs to be integrated has to be embedded into a business environment, the surrounding business processes have to be known. The basis for this is the **business system model**, which we constructed and described in Chapter 3, *Modeling Business Systems*. In order for an IT system to cooperate efficiently with other IT systems, interfaces have to be generated—to in-house IT systems, as well as to the IT systems of other organizations.

In this chapter, we will discuss how to model the messages that are exchanged between the various IT systems, and the processes that are necessary to exchange these messages.

5.1 Terminology of System Integration

Interfaces

Communication between IT systems occurs through **interfaces**. Therefore, an interface is the basic element of system integration. Through an interface, an IT system (the sender) sends information to another IT system (the receiver). A particular IT system can be both a sender and a receiver.

Messages

IT systems that are connected via interfaces exchange **messages**. A message is sent by the sender IT system, with the expectation that receiving the message—immediately or later—initiates an activity in the receiver IT system. For the receiver IT system, each message received constitutes an event to which it responds.

For instance, if an invoice is sent in an electronic format, this event is an **invoice receipt** for the receiver of the invoice. After the receipt of the invoice, the receiver has a certain time frame to pay the bill. The receiver IT system has to confirm the receipt of the invoice and possibly activate another IT system, for example, an accounting system that records the balance.

Messages can be loaded with additional information that is necessary to process the activities of the receiver system. Generally, this information is structured data with defined semantics, such as invoice data or a passenger list. In UN/EDIFACT, for instance, this information is called **reference data**.

Furthermore, messages have assigned control and routing information, for example, sender address, receiver address, meta-information about the content of the message, or checksums. We can also describe this information as the 'packaging' of a message.

There are various alternatives to transform these three components: event, information, and control and reference data, into a message that can be exchanged between IT systems. Control information can, for instance, be 'hidden' in interface programs, or can be sent as additional data. An event can be a program call, or it can be transferred in a file that contains further message data.

In UN/EDIFACT messages, which are also referred to as business documents, all three components are contained in one single transfer unit (mainly data): event (message type), information (reference data), and control information (service segments).

Messages that are sent in XML format are also called documents in XML. They contain at least reference data and meta-information. A great advantage of XML compared to UN/EDIFACT is that each XML message carries with it a reference to its structural description. This has the advantage that everyone can read the XML message.

Enterprise Application Integration

Enterprise Application Integration (EAI) incorporates methods, concepts, and tools for the classification, connection, and coordination of applications within organizations. The goal is integrated business processing by a network of in-house applications of different generations and architectures. This network constantly changes through upgrades or the adding of new applications, through modified technology and other influences.

One of the prerequisites for reaching this goal is the documentation of business processes, of the application network, of the individual applications, and their interfaces, which should be as unified in form and display as possible.

UML is almost perfect for this task. (OMG has created a profile *UML Profile for Enterprise Activation Integration* for this, which explains the technical implementation (conversion etc.) on the basis of UML.)

Electronic Data Interchange

The term **Electronic Data Interchange (EDI)** is a synonym for the standardized exchange of business documents (order, delivery, invoice, shipping information, etc.) between the IT systems of organizations and institutions, such as suppliers or the customs authority. Business documents are also referred to as messages.

The generic term EDI today includes older standards such as **Society for Worldwide Interbank Financial Telecommunication (SWIFT)**, UN/EDIFACT, and ANSI X12. With the development of the Internet, the new standard XML was created. Inter-company data exchange, however, is only one aspect of XML; the functionality of XML goes well beyond this. Because of this, XML does not clearly fall under the generic term EDI.

UN/EDIFACT

United Nations/Electronic Data Interchange for Administration, **Commerce**, **and Transport (UN/EDIFACT)** is an international standard for electronic data exchange in administration, economics, and transportation, which includes rules and message types. Within the framework of **United Nations/Economic Commission for Europe (UN/ECE)**, the UNO aimed at supporting global commerce with electronic tools. In several places throughout this chapter, we will refer to UN/EDIFACT. There are several reasons for this:

- UN/EDIFACT provides the option to depict complex hierarchical message structures. It also contains all three components of a message in one transfer unit: event, reference data, and control information. This makes UN/EDIFACT, conceptually, one of the most sophisticated standards in today's world.

- The UN/EDIFACT standard is available on the Internet and can be used free of charge. (All specifications, regulations, and message types for the UN/EDIFACT standard can be downloaded from `http://www.unece.org/trade/untdid/welcome.htm`.)

XML

The functionality of **eXtensible Markup Language** (**XML**) largely exceeds the field of EDI. EDI is only one of many areas of application of XML and is referred to as XML/EDI. XML can be used *within* as well as *between* organizations.

The XML standard is standardized and published by **World Wide Web Consortium** (the **W3C** `http://www.w3.org`). XML includes many other standards, such as **eXtensible Stylesheet Language** (**XSL**) for the representation of data or Xlink for standardized links. (The XSL family is a collection of recommendations on how XML documents should be transformed and formatted, consisting of three parts: XSLT, Xpath, and XSL-FO: see `http://www.w3c.org/style/XSL`. With the eXML Linking Language contents from various documents can be linked to each other. This will be an essential part of future system integration tools.) XML evolved much quicker than UN/EDIFACT did, and the use of XML as format for data exchange became accepted in a 'bottom-up' manner; the call for standards came much later.

5.2 Messages in UML

In the UML sequence diagram, messages are illustrated with an arrow symbol, together with the name of the message and its parameters (if present). In this way, in UML a message is categorically divided into two parts:

- The name of the message specifies the *event*.
- The arguments of the message contain the *information* that is attached to the message, so that the receiver can perform the necessary activities. Control information belongs in this category as well.

We refer to the information that is exchanged as a **business object**, if the information:

- Is coherent
- Is structured
- Covers the requirements for a certain activity (e.g., invoice, passenger list)
- Is self-contained (no in-house reference keys, etc.)
- Outlives individual interactions

In the UML model of system integration, business objects are structured information sent as arguments in a message from a sender to a receiver.

5.3 One Model—Two Views

For the integration of IT systems, we need to define **which** information needs to be exchanged and **how** it will be exchanged. For this reason, the **system integration model** consists of two different views: the **process view** and the **static view**.

In system integration, the main focus is on process steps that are significantly important for the interaction, exchange of messages, between IT systems and/or involved parties. Nevertheless, often process steps are described that do not necessarily exchange messages, but are important for the complete comprehension of the process. An example of this could be the unloading of the luggage of passengers who did not board the airplane (action **unload luggage** in the activity **no boarding**).

The **static view** describes the **content** and **structure** of the business objects that are exchanged between partners.

The views we use for the system integration model and the UML diagrams within each view are illustrated in Figure 5.1:

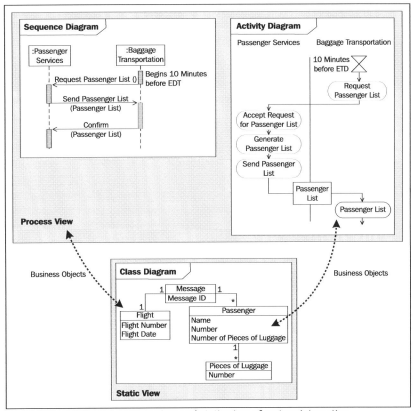

Figure 5.1 Process view and static view of system integration

5.4 Process View

The **process view** depicts those **activities** that an IT system passes through when it exchanges messages with other IT systems. Purely technical processes that are necessary for communication between IT systems, such as dial-up or other connection to the Internet, are not the subject of the process view of our model.

Try to answer the following questions:

- Which activities are we concerned with in the process view? Which interactions exist in our case study between the passenger services system and other IT systems?

- Are these activities only interesting for system integration?

- Have these activities already been described anywhere?

5.4.1 The Business System Model as Foundation

The exchange of messages between IT systems occurs on the basis of **business events**. Therefore, the exchange of messages is an activity of a **subordinate business process**.

In the **business system model** from our case study, the IT system that needs to be integrated is located within the business system **passenger services** (see Figure 5.2):

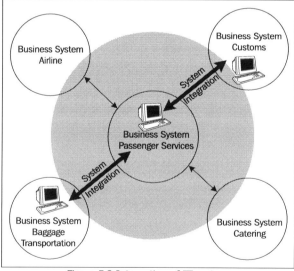

Figure 5.2 Integration of IT system

From the business processes in and around the passenger services business system, all of those business processes that require an interaction between the IT system of our business system and other IT systems are selected. The diagrams constructed for various views of the business model can be used as the foundation for integration.

For the integration with IT systems that belong to the *same* business as the IT system under consideration in our case study passenger services, we use diagrams of the **internal view** of the business system.

For interactions with IT systems that are located *outside* the business system, we use the diagrams of the **external view** of the business system. Here, it is not important whether the external IT systems belong to the same organization or not. For details of the process we can refer to the diagrams of the internal view of the business system.

In our case study we selected two interfaces:

- **Passenger list to customs**: For each flight a passenger list is sent to customs at the destination airport. Each passenger and each crew member is individually mentioned on this list. The transfer of the data takes place through the sending system some time between departure of the plane and arrival at the destination airport. This enables customs at the destination airport to verify the data and to make timely decisions regarding clearance of passengers and crew.

- **No boarding**: Ten minutes before **estimated time** of **departure (ETD)**, the procedure **no boarding** is initiated. This means that ten minutes before EDT, triggered by a timer, baggage transportation requests a passenger list for the corresponding flight. On the passenger services side, the desired passenger list is generated on the receipt of this event. This list specifies all passengers who have not yet boarded the airplane. Once all the luggage of the passengers specified on this list has been unloaded, passenger services receive the passenger list back from baggage transportation, with the appropriate confirmations.

Figure 5.3 shows the use case diagram from Chapter 3, *Modeling Business Systems*, (Figure 3.14), which forms the base diagram for the two marked business use cases.

Both examples include activities from the business use case **requesting passenger list**. The first example, passenger list to customs, describes the interaction between our business system passenger services and the actor **customs of destination airport**, which is marked on the business use case diagram:

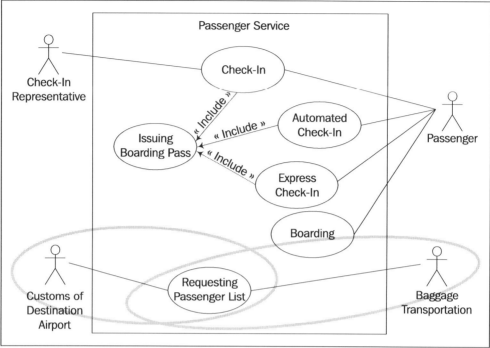

Figure 5.3 Use case diagram of the business system "Passenger Services"

The second example describes the interaction between our business system passenger services and the actor **baggage transportation**, which is also marked on the business use case diagram.

For the description of the process view between involved IT systems, we use the activity diagram and the sequence diagram. For the explanation of the activity diagram and the sequence diagram and for the instructions on reading diagrams we use the example passenger list to customs; for the construction of the diagrams, we use the example no boarding.

5.4.2 Elements of the View

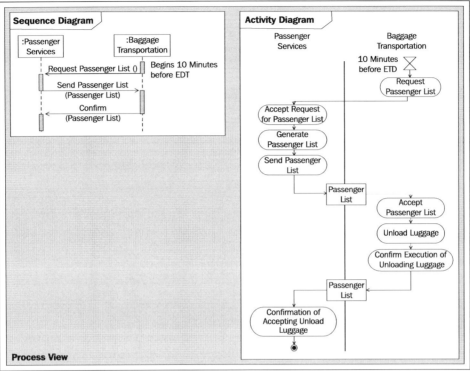

Figure 5.4 Process View

Activities that have to be carried out for the exchange of messages between IT systems can be illustrated well with sequence diagrams and activity diagrams (see Figure 5.4).

- The **activity diagram** describes the flows of actions. The diagram depicts the dependencies between individual actions and the flow of business objects.

- The **sequence diagram** depicts the chronological order of the exchange of messages between the IT systems.

5.4.3 Activity Diagrams

We explained the basic elements of activity diagrams in Section 3.3.5, *Activity Diagrams*. Therefore, here we will only go into the special interpretations and supplemental uses of activity diagrams for system integration.

From the activity diagram in Figure 5.5, we can already extract some initial information for the integration of IT systems for the process **no boarding**. For example, we can learn which business objects are exchanged, etc.

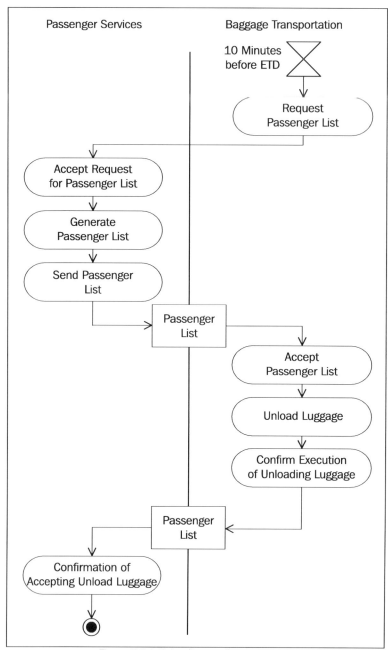

Figure 5.5 Activity diagram "No Boarding"

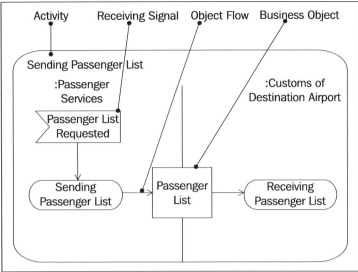

Figure 5.6 Elements of the activity diagram

Activity

In activity diagrams one single activity is depicted as shown in Figure 5.6. In our context, an activity represents a business process. Actions, control elements (decision, branching, merge, start, end, etc.), and objects are essential parts of an activity.

These elements are connected to each other with so-called edges. The connected actions and control elements make up the control flow, which can also be called the **flow**:

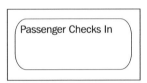

The object flow represents the path of objects that move through the activity. The object flow can also be omitted when constructing activity diagrams. Carrying out an activity can include several parallel flows.

Object Flow (Edge)

Edges, which are depicted as arrows, connect the individual components of the activity diagram and represent the control flow and object flow (edge) of the activity. The control flow determines the flow within an activity.

The incoming arrow starts an individual step of an activity. After this step is completed the flow continues along the outgoing arrow. The object flow describes the flow of objects and data within activities. Edges can be labeled with a name (close to the arrow):

The object flow in an activity diagram shows the path of one or more business objects between the various activities.

Accepting a Signal (Action)

The sending of signals means that a signal is sent to a receiving activity:

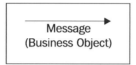

The receiving activity accepts the signal with the action **accepting a signal** and can respond accordingly, meaning, according to the flow that comes from this node in the activity diagram.

Business Object

A business object consists of structured data that is exchanged between actions (see Section 5.2, *Messages in UML*). Generally, the business object that is the output of one action is simultaneously the input of another action:

A business object that leaves its original activity partition is sent from one IT system to another IT system.

Reading Activity Diagrams

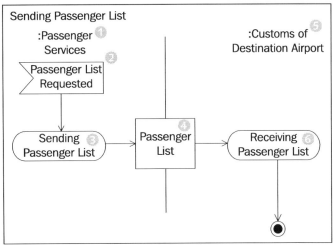

Figure 5.7 Activity diagram

Activity diagrams show the interaction between the various IT systems that are involved in the message exchange. Figure 5.7 shows that the IT system of **passenger services** (1) initiates the action sending **passenger list** (3) through the event **passenger list requested** (2), and that the business object **passenger list** (4) is sent to the IT system of **customs at destination airport** (5). The IT system of customs at the destination airport accepts the **passenger list** (4) with the action **receiving passenger list** (6).

In this diagram, we cannot see that the business object passenger list is sent as the argument of a message. In order to see this, we need to use a sequence diagram.

5.4.4 Sequence Diagram

The focus of sequence diagrams lies in the illustration of the chronological sequence of message exchange between objects as shown in Figure 5.8. The system integration model illustrates the message exchange between IT systems:

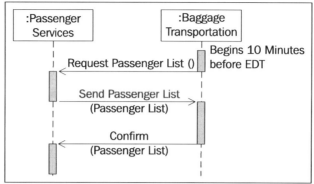

Figure 5.8 Sequence diagram "No Boarding"

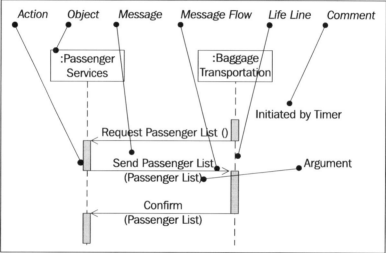

Figure 5.9 Elements of the sequence diagram

In sequence diagrams as shown in Figure 5.9 we work with the following elements:

Object

Objects exchange messages with each other. In the system integration model, these objects represent the interacting IT systems:

Message

In sequence diagrams, messages are understood as operations of events. Information is transferred as arguments:

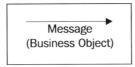

Arguments can be business objects (see Section 5.2, *Messages in UML*).

Message Flow

The message flow goes from the sender of the message to the receiver. In the system integration model, the message flow of the sequence diagram corresponds to the object flow of the activity diagram:

However, the sequence diagram adds the chronological aspect.

Argument

See *Message* above.

Reading Sequence Diagrams

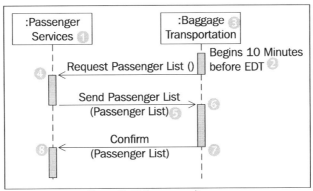

Figure 5.10 Sequence diagram

Figure 5.10 shows that as soon as the prerequisite (2) is fulfilled, baggage transportation requests a passenger list from passenger services (1). Passenger services accepts (4) the request, generates the passenger list, and sends the passenger list back to baggage transportation (6).

On the basis of the passenger list (5), which is received (6) by baggage transportation (3), the affected pieces of luggage are unloaded. Once the luggage has been unloaded, baggage transportation sends an appropriate confirmation to passenger services, by sending a list of passengers whose luggage has been unloaded (7). Finally, passenger services confirm (8) that the luggage has been unloaded. In the sequence diagram, we cannot see what actions are actually performed so that messages can be exchanged. This information is contained in the activity diagram (see Figure 5.11). The individual actions can also be inserted into the sequence diagram as comments; however, this carries the risk of decreasing the readability of the sequence diagram. Unlike activity diagrams, sequence diagrams enable us to see that the business object passenger list is sent as the argument of a message.

5.4.5 Constructing Diagrams in the Process View

To construct diagrams in the process view, we chose the interface to baggage transportation from our case study.

The following checklist shows the necessary steps from constructing activity diagrams and sequence diagrams in the process view:

Checklist 5.1 Constructing Diagrams in the Process View:

- Determine interfaces—Between which IT systems should communication take place?

- Identify involved systems—Which IT systems exchange information?

- Identify activities and control flow—What has to be done and who is responsible for it?

- Define messages—Which messages have to be exchanged?

- Define rules—What influences actions?

- Verify the view—Is everything correct?

Determine Interfaces—Between Which IT Systems Should Communication Take Place?

To carry out the activity **no boarding** (Figure 5.11) those business processes or business use cases that require an interaction with the IT system of passenger services in order to be processed are chosen from the business system model (Chapter 3). In our case study, this applies to the use case **request passenger list**, which has an interface each to baggage transportation and customs at the destination airport. To illustrate the following steps, we will look at the interface to baggage transportation (see Figure 5.3).

We select the actions from the activity **no boarding** that are connected to the exchange of messages:

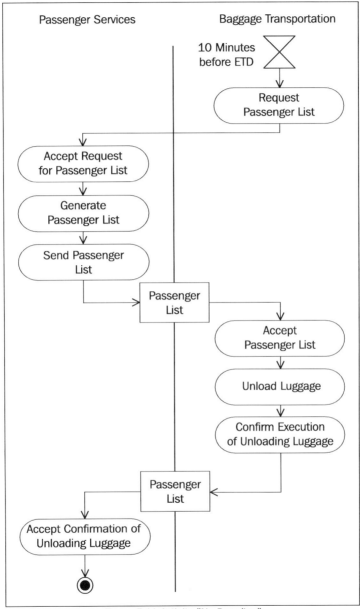

Figure 5.11 Activity "No Boarding"

On the basis of Figure 5.11, we identify the following actions:

- Request passenger list
- Accept request for passenger list
- Generate passenger list
- Send passenger list
- Accept passenger list
- Confirm execution of unloading luggage
- Accept confirmation of unloading luggage

From the sequence diagram of the business model in Figure 5.8, we can see that the following two messages are exchanged:

- **Send passenger list** (passenger list)
- **Confirm** (passenger list)

Identify Involved Systems—Which IT Systems Exchange Information?

In order for messages to be sent and received, it has to be known which IT systems are involved and what roles they play:

- Which IT systems are needed for the execution of business processes? Certainly, our **passenger services** IT system (1) is involved. The IT systems outside the business system can be derived from the actors of the use case diagram of the business model. This is how we found the IT system of the actor **baggage transportation** (2) in our case study, as shown in Figure 5.12:

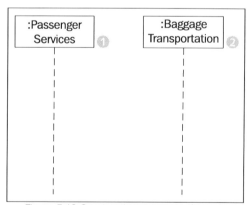

Figure 5.12 Constructing sequence diagram

- Which IT system initiates the process? The process initiator is **baggage transportation** (2).

Independently from the boarding of passenger services, a timer within baggage transportation (set to 10 minutes before EDT), requests a passenger list of passengers who have not yet boarded, so that the unloading of luggage can take place.

- Which IT system is at the end of the process? In our case study, the activity **no boarding** is completed when **passenger services** (1) receive a message from **baggage transportation** that all luggage from passengers who are not yet on board has been unloaded from the plane.

With this information we can start constructing the activity diagram (Figure 5.13):

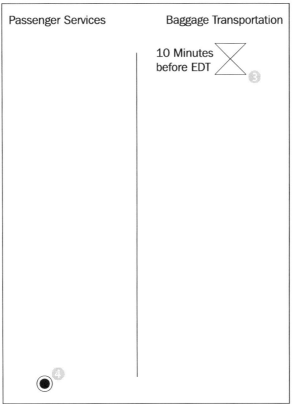

Figure 5.13 Constructing activity diagram

Identify Activities and Control Flow—What has to be Done and Who is Responsible for It?

The following questions will help identify actions and the control flow:

- What needs to be done so that the IT system can exchange messages?

- In which order are activities processed?
- Are there actions that occur simultaneously?
- Which conditions have to be met for the execution of actions?
- Do all prior actions have to be completed before the next one can be completed?
- Who is responsible for processing the actions? In which partition do the actions belong?

The action ...	...is processed by actor...
Request passenger list (1)	Baggage transportation
Accept request for passenger list (2)	Passenger services
Send passenger list (3)	Passenger services
Accept passenger list (4)	Baggage transportation
Confirm execution of unloading luggage (5)	Baggage transportation
Accept confirmation of unloading luggage (6)	Passenger services

This information is documented in the sequence diagram in Figure 5.14 and in the activity diagram in Figure 5.15:

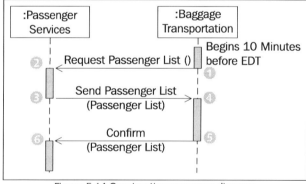

Figure 5.14 Constructing sequence diagram

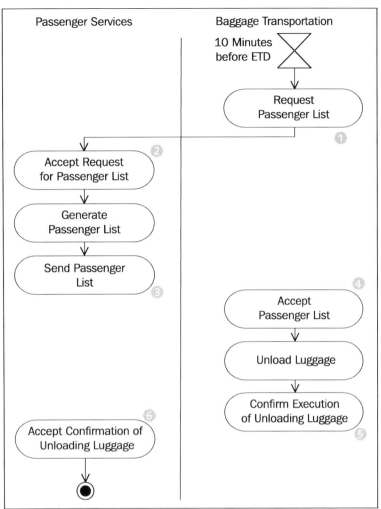

Figure 5.15 Constructing activity diagram

Define Messages—Which Messages have to be Exchanged?

We can see in the business system model that two messages are exchanged:

- **Send passenger list** (passenger list)
- **Confirm** (passenger list)

In the first message **send passenger list** in Figure 5.16, a **passenger list** (7) is sent to the IT system of **baggage transportation** (2), which lists all passengers who have checked in, but have not yet boarded the airplane.

Once the affected pieces of luggage have been unloaded, **passenger services** (1) receive a **confirmation** (5). With the confirmation, the **passenger list** (8) is sent back to **passenger services** (1).

Both messages receive the **passenger list** (7) (8) as argument. In our case, the passenger list was forwarded from **passenger services** (1) to **baggage transportation** (2), modified there, and sent back to **passenger services** (1).

At the end, the passenger list is not exactly the same as it was at the beginning of the activity. However, the **structure** of the business object, Passenger List, remains the same:

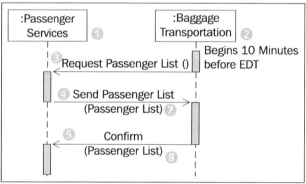

Figure 5.16 Constructing sequence diagram

You can see in Figure 5.17 that the object flow, which runs just like the control flow, hides the control flow:

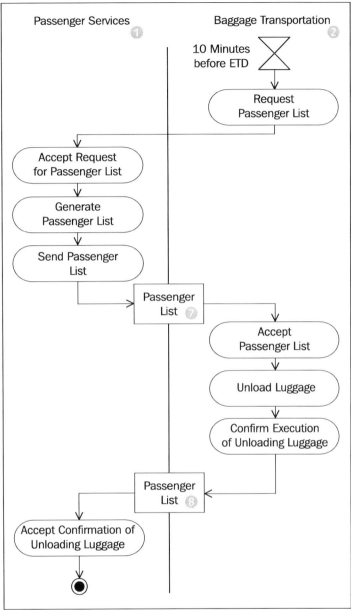

Figure 5.17 Constructing activity diagram

Define Rules—What Influences Actions?

Generally, contracts exist for inter-organization message exchange, which record agreements about responsibilities, regulations, etc. International treaties and statutes further influence this kind of message exchange. On the technical as well as statutory level, standards committees regulate rules about data exchange. (As an example, we recommend the relevant specification *Collaboration-Protocol Profile and Agreement Specification Version 2.0* by ebXML found at `http://ebxml.org/specs/ebcpp-2.0.pdf`.)

As another example, we want to mention **International Air Transport Association (IATA)**, which among other things defines messages and their uses for the entire aerospace industry. Such agreements are also becoming more frequent within organizations. The question is:

- Which agreements, contracts, and statutes have to be taken into consideration for the definition of data exchange?

Verify the View—Is Everything Correct?

Completed sequence diagrams and activity diagrams can be verified with the following checklist:

Checklist 5.2 Verifying Sequence Diagram in the Process View:

- Are all messages that require confirmation listed with a confirmation in the sequence diagram?

- Is every IT system/every business partner that is involved in the exchange of messages listed in at least one sequence diagram?

- Are all exchanged business objects listed in the sequence diagrams as message arguments?

- Are all important comments inserted into the diagram? Are there perhaps too many comments inserted into the diagram, which reduce the clarity of the diagram?

- Does the message flow correspond to the object flow in the activity diagram?

Checklist 5.3 Verifying Activity Diagrams in the Process View:

- When you construct activity diagrams in the process view, remember that only the flows that are involved in the message exchange are relevant. Business processes belong in the business model.

- Is the object flow clearly visible? Are all business objects listed in the activity diagram?

- The conditions of different outputs should not overlap. Otherwise, the control flow is ambiguous, meaning that it is not clear where the flow proceeds at a decision node.

- The conditions must include all possibilities. Otherwise, the control flow can get stuck. In case of doubt, insert an output with the condition "else".

- Forks and joins should be well balanced. The number of flows that leave a fork should match the number of flows that end in the corresponding join.

5.5 The Static View

The static view describes the structure of business objects that are sent as message arguments from the sender to the receiver of the message (also see Section 5.2, *Messages in UML*).

The following points should be taken into consideration when modeling business objects:

- It is important to pay attention to *semantic integrity*. The structure and content of business objects have to be clear and easy to understand for all involved parties.

- Information has to be coherent and all involved parties should be able to interpret it.

- Business objects should be reusable.

- Business objects have to be complete, so that they satisfy even rarely occurring demands and there is no room for ambiguity.

Different requirements and different modeling approaches lead to different structures of business objects. It is not possible to fulfill all demands simultaneously. The structure and scope of a business object is *always* a compromise; the ideal business object can never be found.

5.5.1 Elements of the View

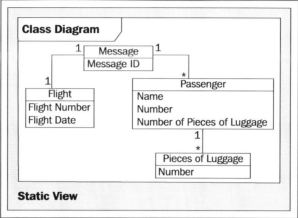

Figure 5.18 Static view

For the illustration of business objects in the static view of the system integration model, we only use the class diagram, as illustrated in Figure 5.18.

5.5.2 Class Diagram

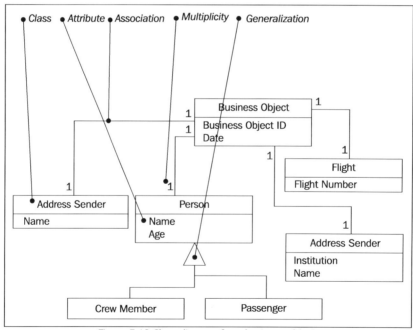

Figure 5.19 Class diagram for a business object

For a more detailed discussion of class modeling, see Chapter 4 Section 4.2, *Structural View*. Below, we will only explain the specifics of the system integration model.

Class

A class in the class diagram (Figure 5.19) of the system integration model represents a coherent set of information, which is contained in a business object:

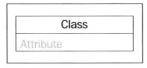

Reading Class Diagrams

Reading class diagrams of business objects is no different from reading class diagrams of IT systems. For this see Chapter 4 Section 4.2.5, *Class Diagram*.

5.5.3 Constructing Class Diagrams

The following checklist shows the necessary steps for constructing class diagrams of business objects. Subsequently, we will explain the individual steps further.

Checklist 5.4 Constructing Class Diagrams of the Static View:

- Collect information relevant for the business objects—What do we want to read?

- Construct class diagram—What is the structure of the business object?

- Adopt classes and attributes from the class diagram of the IT system—What is present in the class diagram?

- Derive remaining data elements—From where do I get the rest?

- Define classes and relationships of the business object—Which class relationships do we need?

- Verify the view—Is everything correct?

Collect Information Relevant for the Business Objects—What Do We Want to Read?

In the top-down approach, business processes are the foundation for the modeling of business objects. On the basis of these business processes, we define the *information* that has to be exchanged in order for a business process to be executed.

From this, we derive the structure and content of the **business objects**. The advantage of this approach is that IT system specifics do not contaminate modeling results. The modeled business objects become independent of the IT system, and therefore, reusable. However, linking them to the IT system often requires more effort.

The top-down approach creates business objects that can be used by many different types of IT systems. The standardized EDI messages of inter-enterprise data exchange are modeled according to this approach.

If an existing IT system serves as the foundation for modeling business objects, content can be derived from the classes of the IT system. It is not always possible to derive all information from the underlying IT system. Values that are important for a business object are not necessarily relevant for the underlying IT system. An example for this is the number of pieces of luggage that a passenger checks in: in the business object this information is attached as a control element, but in the IT system this information is meaningless. The class diagram of the IT system depicts the information from another perspective than the one we need for the class diagram of the business object. In turn, internal identification characteristics that serve the identification of objects within IT systems are out of place in a system-spanning business object.

Where a standard is mandatory for a business object, we use standard messages from the appropriate catalogue. (On this topic, also see UN/ECE, `http://www.unece.org`; ebXML, `http://wwwebxml.org`; and many other industry-specific suppliers of messages.) Even when standard messages do not have to be used, taking a look at these catalogues can be worth it. The content of standard messages can make suggestions for the content of the business objects that you need to design.

The following question should be asked when designing business objects:

- What is the minimum information that the receiving IT system needs in order to perform its work?

Applied to the case study the question is:

- What is the minimum information that baggage transportation needs on the passenger list, in order to unload the luggage of passengers who did not board the airplane?

We can obtain this information by interviewing knowledge carriers from baggage transportation:

- The flight number, date, and time of scheduled departure, so that the correct plane will be unloaded
- The numbers of labels that are attached to the pieces of luggage of passengers who did not board the airplane

Construct Class Diagram—What is the Structure of the Business Object?

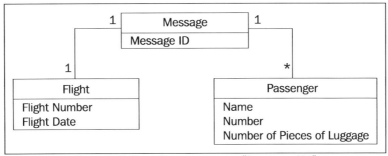

Figure 5.20 Class diagram message "Passenger List"

Figure 5.20 shows the class model for the message **passenger list**. With this model we can deliver the data that baggage transportation needs. This model serves as the goal model for the transformation of data from the IT system.

Adopt Classes and Attributes from the Class Diagram of the IT System—What is Present in the Class Diagram?

Since the business object has to be created by the sender IT system, we first examine the class diagram of the IT system as source. The question is:

- Which data elements of the business object can be created from the class diagram of the IT system?

In the case study, the answer looks like this (in order to make the attribution to classes of the IT system visible, we chose the notation **classname.attribute**):

- Flight number: **flightnumber.description**
- Date and time of scheduled flight: **flight.flightdate**
- Number of passenger: **ticket.number**
- Name of passenger: **customer.name**

Derive Remaining Data Elements—From Where Do I Get the Rest?

For all the data elements of the business object that cannot be generated directly from the class diagram of the IT system, we have to find another solution. The question is:

- How can we derive the data elements that we cannot generate directly from the class diagram?

In the case study, the following data elements cannot be derived from the IT system:

- **Clear identification of the business object**: There are several possibilities. For example, we can use serial numbers or semantically comprehensible keys that are unambiguous (flight number with date and time). In our example, two options can be used:

- **Flight number with date and time of the scheduled departure**: This data is available in the IT system.

- **Unique serial number**: A unique serial number is usually generated during the creation of the business object and is not part of the class diagram of the IT system.

- **Passenger's number of pieces of luggage**: Information about the number of pieces of luggage that a passenger checked in is not available in the class diagram of the IT system. By counting the number of objects in the class **piece of luggage** of a certain passenger, the number of pieces of luggage can be determined.
  This information is important for the business object, because in the case **no boarding** it provides the opportunity to check in a simple manner whether all pieces of luggage have been unloaded.

- **Sender/Receiver**: Especially for the exchange of data between business partners it is necessary to attach additional pieces of information to the message, in order to identify it later. Generally, these are sender and receiver identification, message ID (see above), time that the message was sent, etc. In the passenger list PAXLST, for instance, a person who is responsible for the message's content has to be named.

Define Classes and Relationships of the Business Object— Which Class Relationships do We Need?

In the class diagram of the business object, relationships among classes have to be defined. The questions are:

- How can we derive classes and relationships from the business model? The class diagram of the business model contains business objects. In our case study, **passenger list** is part of the class diagram of the business system **passenger services**. From the description of the business object in the business model, we can derive classes, attributes, and relationships for modeling the business object as part of the message.

In addition to the classes that contain necessary data, we often also use classes that enable the connection between the needed classes within the IT system. In our example, Figure 5.20, we also have to consider the classes **coupon** and **ticket**, otherwise, we cannot accomplish a connection between flight and passengers.

- How can we derive data and relationships from other standard messages? We can adopt data elements or data element groups from existing standard messages that have identical or similar content. UN/EDIFACT, for instance, provides us with so-called standard segments (data element groupings) that contain information such as **name and address** or **receiver information**. Even if the UN/EDIFACT standard is not applied, we can use classes, relationships, and attributes from these segments and data elements as a blueprint for the business object.

- How can we transform classes from the IT system into the business object? As we mentioned above, the classes of a business object can be derived in part or even completely from the classes of the IT system. Since the requirements on the classes of the IT system are different from the requirements on the classes of the business object, a transformation of classes and attributes from the IT system into the business object becomes necessary.

Figure 5.21 shows the class diagram of the passenger services IT system. As examples for the transformation steps, we will transform the data concerning flight and passengers on the basis of this class diagram, or rather show how they should be transformed. However, we have left the necessary activities for the transformation of the various types and formats of data completely unconsidered in this example. You can find more information to this topic in *UML Profile for Enterprise Application Integration* at http://www.omg.org/technology/documents/formal/eai.htm.

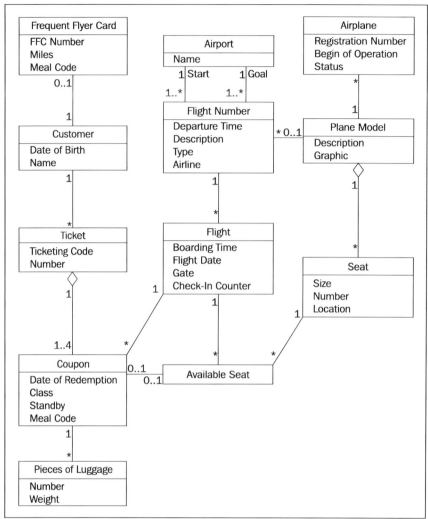

Figure 5.21 Class diagram of the IT system "Passenger Services"

Verify the View—Is Everything Correct?

The completed class diagram can be verified with the following checklist:

Checklist 5.5 Verifying Class Diagrams in the Static View:

- Is the class diagram complete? Does the business object contain all the information, so that sender and receiver can carry out their activities?

- Did you check that the business object contains only data elements that can be interpreted by outsiders?

- Did you check whether it is possible to use standard messages?

- Are the relationships labeled in a meaningful manner? Are the directions of the arrows correct?

- Is the class diagram correct? Intensive reading of the class diagram together with knowledge carriers and running through each scenario will bring most mistakes to light.

5.5.4 Transforming Data from the IT System to the Message "passenger list"

On the basis of the available class diagrams of passenger services and the message passenger list, we will explain the necessary steps for selecting and transforming data concerning flight and passengers.

In Figure 5.22, we have emphasized the classes needed for the transformation of flight and passenger data, or rather, de-emphasized the classes of the diagram that we do not need:

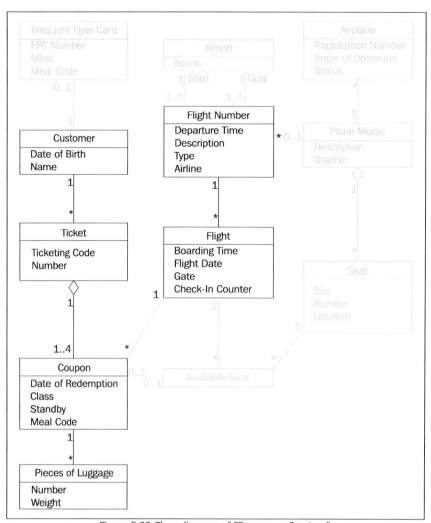

Figure 5.22 Class diagram of "Passenger Services"

Transformation of Flight Data

We can see in Figure 5.23 that a **flight** has *n* corresponding flights. The multiplicity of the class flight is insignificant, since we are only interested in an exactly 1:1 relationship for each message—meaning, we are only interested in one single flight at a time. In the business object, the two classes of the IT system can be combined to one class, and attributes relevant for the business object can be adopted:

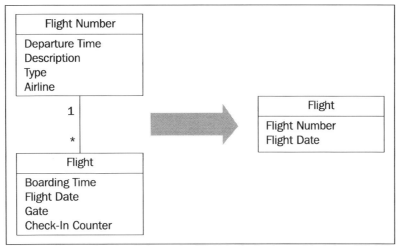

Figure 5.23 Transforming flight number/flight to the business object class "Flight"

To obtain the correct message data from the IT system, we have to indicate the day of the desired flight as selection criterion in addition to the flight number.

Transformation of Passenger Data

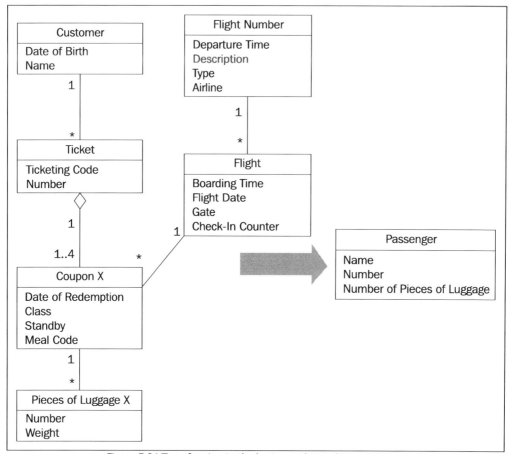

Figure 5.24 Transforming to the business object class passenger

For the transformation of passenger data to the message **passenger list**, we need many more steps than we did for the flight data.

Define which data is needed:

- **customer.name**
- **ticket.number**
- count (**piece of luggage**)

Regulations define how the correct data can be read out of the IT system. In addition to the rules about how to read the necessary data from the various classes, we have to ensure that only passengers who belong on the selected flight, and who also are on board this flight, are listed.

5.5.5 Transformation of UML Messages into Various Standard Formats

All standard formats for data exchange, whether ebXML, SWIFT, or UN/EDIFACT, have their own way of **structuring** and **representing** messages. SWIFT messages are described not only graphically, but also with text. The same is true for UN/EDIFACT, where the graphic illustrations are standardized through the use of branching diagrams.

The trend is clearly going into the direction of modeling messages in a fundamentally protocol and implementation neutral way, with UML.

Then all the standard formats can be derived from the representation in UML, the "mother of all messages". Depending on availability this can even be done according to firmly defined transformation rules. (The profile *UML Profile for Enterprise Distributed Object Computing* was developed as guidelines for the translation of UML descriptions into 'real' business systems. This profile, in turn, is based upon standards of ebXML.) Some of the arguments for choosing UML as a neutral form of representation are:

- System-and implementation-independent description of business objects and messages
- Accepted and widely used standard
- Option of depicting messages and business processes
- Unified language for the description of systems

An essential advantage of neutral message specification in UML is the much easier conversion of messages from one format to another. Because of this, we recommend the modeling of messages in UML first, and subsequently transforming messages into the appropriate format. Here, it is not important whether the target format is a standard format or an in-house proprietary format. Especially in the later case, it is much easier to convert a project from a proprietary format to a standard one if neutral UML specifications are available.

A detailed description of transformation rules would go well beyond the scope of this text. Because of this, we would like to refer to OMG's **Model Driven Architecture** (**MDA** http://www.omg.org/mda/) and the two profiles *UML Profile for Enterprise Distributed Object Computing* (www.omg.org/technology/documents/formal/edoc.htm) and *UML Profile for Enterprise Application Integration* (http://www.omg.org/technology/documents/formal/eai.htm), which provide comprehensive insight into this subject matter from a UML perspective.

Index

Thank you for buying UML 2.0 in Action A Project-Based Tutorial

Writing for Packt

We welcome all inquiries from people who are interested in authoring. Book proposals should be sent to authors@packtpub.com. If your book idea is still at an early stage and you would like to discuss it first before writing a formal book proposal, contact us: one of our commissioning editors will get in touch with you.

We're not just looking for published authors; if you have strong technical skills but no writing experience, our experienced editors can help you develop a writing career, or simply get some additional reward for your expertise.

About Packt Publishing

Packt, pronounced 'packed,' published its first book "*Mastering phpMyAdmin for Effective MySQL Management*" in April 2004 and subsequently continued to specialize in publishing highly focused books on specific technologies and solutions.

Our books and publications share the experiences of your fellow IT professionals in adapting and customizing today's systems, applications, and frameworks. Our solution-based books give you the knowledge and power to customize the software and technologies you're using to get the job done. Packt books are more specific and less general than the IT books you have seen in the past. Our unique business model allows us to bring you more focused information, giving you more of what you need to know, and less of what you don't.

Packt is a modern, yet unique publishing company, which focuses on producing quality, cutting-edge books for communities of developers, administrators, and newbies alike. For more information, please visit our website: www.packtpub.com.

More *solutions* Less *wasted time*

Learning eZ publish 3

Leaders of the eZ publish community guide you through this complex and powerful PHP-based content management system.

- Build content rich websites and applications using eZ publish
- Discover the secrets of the eZ publish templating system
- Develop the skills to create new eZ publish extensions

Building Websites with the ASP.NET Community Starter Kit

A comprehensive guide to understanding, implementing and extending the powerful and freely available application from Microsoft.

- Learn .NET architecture through building real-world examples
- Understand, implement, and extend the Community Starter Kit
- Learn to create and customize your own website
- For ASP.NET developers with a sound grasp of C#

Building Websites with OpenCms

A practical guide to understanding and working with this proven Java/JSP based content management system.

- Understand how OpenCms handles and publishes content to the Web
- Learn how to create your own complex, OpenCms website
- Develop the skills to implement, customize, and maintain an OpenCms website

SpamAssassin: A practical guide to Configuration, Customization, and Integration

An in-depth guide to implementing antispam solutions using SpamAssassin.

- Detect and prevent spam using SpamAssassin
- Install, configure, and customize SpamAssassin
- Integrate SpamAssassin with major mail agents and antispam services
- Use SpamAssassin to implement the best antispam solution for your network and your business requirement

Content Management with Plone

A comprehensive guide to the Plone content management system for Plone website administrators and developers.

- Design, build, and manage content rich websites using Plone
- Extend Plone's skins and content types
- Customize, secure and optimize Plone websites

Business Process Execution Language for Web Services

An architect and developer's guide to orchestrating web services using BPEL4WS.

- Specification of business processes in BPEL
- BPEL and its relation to other standards
- Advanced BPEL features such as compensation, concurrency, scopes, and correlations
- The Oracle BPEL Process Manager and BPEL Designer
- The Microsoft BizTalk Server 2004 as a BPEL server

Building Websites with Microsoft Content Management Server

A fast-paced and practical tutorial guide for C# developers starting out with MCMS 2002.

- Learn directly from recognized community experts
- Benefit from rapid developer level tutorials
- Develop a feature rich custom site incrementally
- Receive professional tips and tricks from developer newsgroups and online communities

Visit www.packtpub.com for information on all our books.